GREAT RIVERS
of the world

PAOLO NOVARESIO

BARNES & NOBLE

NEW YORK

TABLE OF CONTENTS

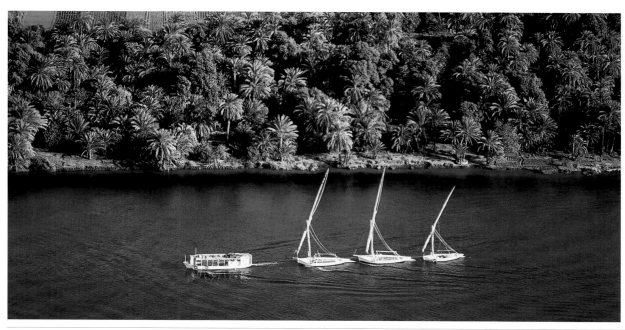

TEXTS
Paolo Novaresio

PROJECT EDITOR
Valeria Manferto De Fabianis

COLLABORATING EDITORS
Laura Accomazzo
Novella Monti

GRAPHIC DESIGN
Paola Piacco

© 2006 by White Star S.p.a.

This 2006 edition published by
Barnes & Noble Publishing, Inc.
by arrangement with White Star S.p.a.

TRANSLATION: RICHARD PIERCE

2006 Barnes & Noble Publishing

ISBN-13: 978-0-7607-8238-5
ISBN-10: 0-7607-8238-5

Library of Congress
Cataloging-in-Publication
Data available

Printed and bound in Korea
Color separation by Chiaroscuro, Turin

1 3 5 7 9 10 8 6 4 2

INTRODUCTION

The dry desert rivers narrate stories to those who walk on their parched beds. We sift the sand underfoot. If the grains are round they are the result of wind erosion; if on the other hand they have an irregular shape that means they have been forged by water. On this kind of terrain it is not always clear that we are on a riverbed and where the river flowed. Only along the banks, which are sometimes miles away, is it easy to envisage the river. Here the water has left what could be called phantom strata: eroded rock, white lines of minerals, smooth hollows and grooves where the current was strong. The direction the creeping plants take tells you the direction of the river.

Rivers never die. It takes only one storm a year in the distant mountains to make a river swell again, if only for one night, with rapidly flowing water. The Tuareg, the shepherds and caravan leaders of the Sahara, have a saying: "Aman, imam," that is, "Water is soul." It does not matter if their rivers have a short life, since what they leave on the sandstone beds provides enough humidity for the vegetation to survive. From above, the dry rivers look like grass and plants flowing in a bed.

In one of these almost green rivulets I met a river genie. It was September, in the Ennedi massif in Chad. The river is called Archeï, which means "place always full of water." I saw only a huge valley with bent acacia trees and fragile bushes, but I knew that upstream the river becomes narrow and flows thread-like through the rocks for a few hundred feet every day of the year. Once the Archeï was a tributary of the immense Bahr el-Ghazal, the River of the Gazelles, which flowed northward parallel to the Nile, exiting from huge Lake Chad. Today, along this dry river, a few semi-nomadic people eke out a living on the dead sand dunes, while the lake is now a mere pool. However, rather recently – a thousand years ago and then in the 17th-18th century – the Bahr el-Ghazal once again flowed toward the basins of the northern desert, completely changing the life there. Scientists say that an increase in the level of Lake Chad of 933 feet (283 m) would be enough to make the Ennedi desert an oasis.

But to get back to my encounter, I met a girl there, a member of the Bideyat nomadic tribe, whose name was Aecha. She covered her face with the yellow plant shoots of a small broom she was using to gather tiny, round and almost black grains of wild millet. In two days of raking Aecha had gathered a small conical pile of seeds measuring about 28 by 14 inches (70 x 35 cm). "This year was unusually rainy," she said as soon as we managed to communicate. "The river will give us enough to eat." The great Persian poet Saadi from Shiraz wrote in 1292: "The torrent that rushes headlong from the mountains vanishes in the precipices, but the tiniest drop of dew is absorbed by the sun, which takes it up to the sky."

Despite the fact that all the rivers in the world amount to only a small portion of the 9600 cubic miles (40,000 cubic km) of fresh water available, they are more than mere waterways, for rivers mean kinetic energy. With their descending gradients they also represent potential power, before becoming waterfalls. Like human beings, rivers are born and have different origins. The Rhône River rises from a frozen brook in a glacier; the Volga has a marshy source. Rivers may flow out of an immense lake such as the Angara from Lake Baikal, or from a tiny lake like Itasca, which gives rise to the Mississippi. The headstream may pop out of the side of a mountain, as occurs with the Shenandoah and the Po, or emerge in asymmetrical fashion from a meadow, as does the Thames. And the sources of the Nile remained a mystery for well over 2,000 years, since the time of Herodotus, a mystery that had to be solved at any cost.

According to the dynamics of fluids, flowing water is a complex system that is extremely sensitive to its initial conditions and configuration: there is no system of equations able to describe the motion of a river, nor is it possible to make predictions concerning its course. The tiniest variations at the beginning of the river system produce chaotic behavior in mathematical terms. Rivers attract living organisms and at the same time are barriers. When humankind began to evolve in Africa, first in the forests and then in the savannas, the network of rivers isolated the various groups, accelerating the evolution of our species in a mosaic pattern: erect posture in one area, skillful manipulation in another, and the development of the cranium in yet another one. Then the rivers dried up, or changed course, which eliminated some barriers, thus allowing the groups of humans to produce new mixtures of genes and features.

And it precisely along the rivers (now dry) on the shores of the lakes of Africa that scientists have found fossils of the first humans, some as much as 4,000,000 years old. On the Nariokotome, a brook that empties into Lake Turkana in

Kenya, a specimen of *Homo ergaster*, our fossil ancestor, was found. It was a nine-year-old boy who was extremely tall, 5.25 ft (1.60 m), who would have reached a height of almost 6.6 ft (2 m) had he lived longer. One day some 1.6 million years ago, the boy dragged himself to the river to drink some water. He had a high fever because of an abscess in an upper left molar (clearly seen in the fossil skull), and this is why he died. But the river consoled him by cooling him and then covering him with its sediment. Thanks to the river, the Turkana Boy became immortal as Fossil WT 15000, the most complete skeleton of a hominid ever found.

As often occurs with humans, some rivers flow into dead ends. In southern Africa, the Okavango River, its course altered by earthquakes, does not reach the Zambesi and dies out in an inland delta consisting of millions of small canals with transparent water that is the home of marvelous fauna. Proceeding along its course, the river becomes less powerful, the water slides on the bed rather than eroding it and ends up widening in the flatlands of Makgadikgadi, where the river turns into very white silt. One day, with a group of Bushmen, we tried to get there on foot, stopping beforehand to drink. The Australian Aborigines, on the other hand, have always known how to make use of periodic rivers that furnish the billabongs (temporary wells) around the Gibson Desert with water or, flowing westward from the Great Dividing Range in Queensland, supply the huge Artesian Basin of central Australia with underground water. The billabongs are hallucinatory rivers: they exist and don't exist, but those who are acquainted with totemic practices such as the hunter-gatherer Aborigines, know how to find the ancestor-rivers – and also how to survive.

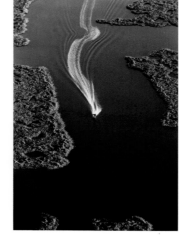

The fact that rivers are part of the mythical universe is demonstrated by the thousands of glass beads (precious for their rarity) that the black Africans have since time immemorial cast into the beds of their rivers. The physical and spiritual energy of rivers has made them a tool of humankind. In keeping with a model of hydraulic society, it was the available supply of water drawn from rivers that generated large empires governed by authoritarian bureaucracies able to make vast areas productive. Architecture became monumental, the political system despotic: both these conditions served the need to keep constantly occupied and under control the huge number of laborers needed to construct and maintain the hydraulic structures. A Sumerian text from 4000 BC says: "Without coercion no city could be founded. The rivers would not come out of their beds." Typical hydraulic societies are the Mesopotamian and Egyptian civilizations, but from Babylon to New York the cities (hence the word "civilization") are situated along rivers and for rivers. It took only 100 years of human labor to shorten the Rhine by 75 miles (120 km).

The Missouri River is an uninterrupted chain of artificial lakes with levees that cannot be eroded: the chaotic movement of the waves is subdued by cement. The present-day construction of at least 500 dams per year means that over 60 percent of the river water in the world is now controlled and regulated by humankind. The concept of thirst is expressed by the Sahara Bedouins, people who wash themselves with sand even for their prayer ablutions (thanks to a special dispensation from Muhammad), as follows: "A man digs a well and finds water. Not satisfied, he continues to dig and finds only ashes."

Alberto Salza

---

1 The Pointe-aux-Alouettes on the St. Lawrence River in Quebec, Canada.

2-3 The east branch of the Nile Delta, between El-Mansura and Damietta, Egypt.

4-5 The Pont des Arts bridge over the Seine, Paris.

6 Aggstein castle on the Danube, Austria.

7 A group of boats navigating on the Nile, Egypt.

9 The Yukon at the confluence with the Porcupine River in Alaska.

10 A strip of land washed by the waters of the Huang He River, China.

11 The bayous, secondary arms of the Mississippi Delta, New Orleans, Louisiana.

12-13 The Colorado River winding through Canyonlands National Park, Utah, U.S.A.

14-15 A stretch of the tortuous course of the Amazon River, Brazil.

EUROPE

With the exception of the Danube, the most important European rivers flow through the large plain that stretches from the Ural Mts. to northern France without being interrupted by mountain ranges. This section of the continent has two major focal points from which rivers radiate: the mountain system that goes from the Alps to the eastern Carpathian Mts., and the hilly area of central Russia. The Volga, Dnepr and Don flow in the immense Sarmatian lowlands: the slight gradient makes these waterways suitable for navigation, but their economic importance is limited by the fact that they empty into enclosed basins such as the Black and Caspian seas.

The rivers that flow into the Atlantic are much more important as commercial routes: the Thames, Seine, Elbe, and above all the Rhine, which can be negotiated by large vessels as far as Basel and the Swiss border. Their deltas, which are exposed to the sea tides, host the main harbors in Europe: Le Havre, London, Hamburg, and Rotterdam can rightly be considered the gateways of the continent.

A network of artificial canals laid out during the Soviet period links the Volga River and the Baltic Sea, the Black Sea and the White Sea. Other canals, as well as a maze of secondary branches, connect the Rhine to the Seine and Danube, thus linking the industrial heart of the new European Union with the outlying and developing areas.

The waterway network in Scandinavia is negligible, since the rivers are either torrential or are mostly links among a multitude of lakes. The rivers on the Mediterranean, where rainfall is slight, generally have a limited discharge and are subject to dramatic low-water periods in the summer. The Ebro, Rhône and the Po – the only really large river in Italy – are the sole exceptions to this rule.

Over the centuries the major Europeans rivers have played the role of frontiers, areas of contact and mediation among different peoples, busy commercial routes, and means of migration. Large urban and industrial areas have risen up along their banks, greatly altering their natural features. Irresponsible exploitation has had grave consequences, such as the catastrophic floods that have afflicted the Po River Valley in the last decade. Until the 1960s the Rhine, Seine and Thames were among the most polluted rivers in the world, veritable open-air sewers. Since then the situation has changed for the better, and the first salmon have reappeared in the Atlantic estuaries, offering hope for the future. It is necessary and possible to live together with rivers. After all, the Europeans have done so for millennia.

16 left A fishing boat goes down one of the branches of the Danube near its mouth, in Romania.

16 center The elegant Chenonceaux château on the Loire, France.

16 right The marshes created by the Po River in the Volano forest in the Emilia-Romagna region of Italy.

17 The Houses of Parliament and the Victoria Tower viewed from the Thames, London, England.

18 About 18 miles (30 km) from its headwaters, near the town of Lechlade, in Gloucestershire, the Thames flows peacefully over a clay bed through bucolic and uncontaminated countryside that has remained virtually the same since the time of ancient Romans and Saxons.

UNITED KINGDOM

Oxford Windsor
London

THE THAMES

THE ALLURE OF NOBILITY

The Thames River rises on the limestone highland of the Cotswold Hills, in Gloucestershire. But where, exactly? For a long time pinpointing the headstreams of the river was the subject of heated discussions between opposing parties. With typically British perseverance the matter was even discussed in Parliament: in 1937 it was officially established that the Thames begins at Thames Head, near the village of Kemble. The fact that the source is almost always dry is wholly secondary. In reality, the true Thames takes shape a few miles farther on, thanks to a series of small headstreams the merge near the town of Cricklade. Compared to the giants of Asia, Africa and America, the longest river in England seems little more than a brook. It is 211 miles (340 km)

long, has a rather modest rate of outflow, no truly important affluents to speak of, and would barely deserve being featured on maps. But for the English the Thames is much more than a waterway, an inland means of communication, or a fine place to spend one's leisure time; it is the very symbol of the nation, the emblem of a lifestyle, of a way of thinking and behaving.

The Thames is above all London, which until the first decades of the 20th century was the largest city in the world and the capital of an empire that ranged from southern Africa to Burma. The river has witnessed all the major events of English history from the time when Caesar's Roman legions laid out a city called Londinium in the mid-1st century BC. Invaders such as the Saxons, Danes and Normans went up the Thames and fought there. The Magna Carta, the first constitution in Europe, which laid the foundation for Western democracy, was signed near the riverbanks. The foggy, tranquil atmosphere of the river inspired painters such as Canaletto and Turner as well as a host of illustrious poets and writers, including Shelley, Dickens, Wilde, Kipling, Lewis Carroll and Kenneth Grahame. Handel sings its praises in his famous Water Music, and Jerome K. Jerome set the exhilarating adventures of his *Three Men in a Boat* there.

From the beginning of its course the Thames is fraught with fascination and memories. At Lechlade, about 19 miles (30 km) from the sources, the river becomes navigable thanks to a series of locks. Today most of the river traffic in this section consists of pleasure craft, but once the wharves of Lechlade hosted the large barges that went from London to the upper course of the Thames and vice versa, laden with all kinds of cargo. The dome of St. Paul's Cathedral in London was built with Lechlade stone.

Winding lazily through hills and green fields, the Thames

18-19 Meadows, woods and cultivated fields flank the Thames on its journey through the open countryside of Gloucestershire, in the vicinity of Kempsford. Fortunately, urbanization has spared the banks of the river, which are the home of isolated farmhouses and quaint villages.

19 bottom The sleepy town of Lechlade, on the banks of the Thames, was once a lively river port used as a landing place by the barges laden with cargo transported from London. Nowadays Lechlade is basically a resort town frequented by pleasure-craft enthusiasts.

20-21 The ancient city of Oxford, situated at the confluence of the Thames and the Cherwell, is world famous for its prestigious university. The Bodleian Library, founded in 1450, is extremely interesting; it boasts a collection of over 1,500,000 books and precious manuscripts.

20 bottom In the vicinity of the town of Goring, in Oxfordshire, the Thames penetrates a gorge that lies between Berkshire Downs and the Chiltern Hills and then winds its way into a valley and heads toward London through a region that was once marshy and with few roads.

21 top The town of Henley-on-Thames, founded in the 12th century on the north bank of the Thames in Oxfordshire, was formerly an important trade center and has noteworthy monuments and vestiges of the past.

21 bottom In the idyllic setting of Oxfordshire the Thames is at its loveliest: the evocative landscapes created by the slow and tortuous flow of the river inspired poets and writers such as Shelley, Jerome K. Jerome and Lewis Carroll, the author of the famous novel Alice's Adventures in Wonderland.

THE THAMES

moves toward Oxford and its junction with the Cherwell. In this section nothing disturbs the placid flow of the river as it runs through a bucolic countryside that has been the same for centuries. Oxford is one of the most beautiful and interesting cities in Europe; its monumental university, the oldest in England, was founded in the 1200s and now has 39 colleges. Lacking in the list of illustrious figures who graduated from Oxford is Shelley: he was expelled for having published the pamphlet *The Necessity of Atheism*, which triggered a scandal. At Oxford, tradition is taken seriously and must be respected in all its aspects, including the rivalry with Cambridge both in the field of study and rowing races. Almost every year since 1829 the two universities have met in the historic boat race, traditionally rowed between Putney and Mortlake, where the Thames iis broad but also has a bend. The race, held in spring attracts thousands of fans, who are packed along the riverside and also on any available craft on the river itself.

One of the favorite pastimes of the English is to navigate on punts, the typical boats propelled by poles; men with straw hats and women dressed in white and armed with the inevitable parasol make one think of the past and the Thames as described by Jerome. Between Oxford and Windsor the idylls between the river and English literature become even more passionate: every bend, every meander under the shade of willow trees, and every village preserves moving and poetic memories. It seems that Jerome K. Jerome got the idea for his most famous book in a pub at Clifton Hampden, in the vicinity of Oxford, in 1889.

The setting for the story of the three men and the dog that go up the Thames – plagued by a myriad humorous complications – for a vacation in contact with Mother Nature, was well known to the author, who spent most of his life along the river. And Lewis Carroll's *Alice's Adventures in Wonderland* was conceived during a boat trip he took to entertain the young daughter of a friend of his.

THE THAMES

22 top and center Every year since 1829, with rare exceptions, the Thames has been the venue of the famous Oxford vs Cambridge boat race.

22 bottom Trips down the river on the characteristic punts, small boats propelled by a long pole, are one of the favorite pastimes of the Oxford University students. One of the most popular is the ride from Magdalen College down the Cherwell River as far as its confluence with the Thames at Folly Bridge.

22-23 A bridge with five arches built in 1786 connects the opposite banks of the Thames at Henley-on-Thames, in Oxfordshire. A museum dedicated to the river and to the sport of rowing reveals the strong, centuries-old relationship this town has with the Thames.

24 top The village of Marlow, in Buckinghamshire, has always been linked with great romantic poet Percy Bysshe Shelley, who lived there with his second wife Mary.

24 bottom left Reading, Berkshire's county town and the only industrial city in the middle course of the Thames, has many cultural institutions and a famous university.

24 bottom right Time seems to have come to a halt at

Mapledurham, which is the historic home of the Blount family and the last watermill in operation on the Thames River.

24-25 Hampton Court Palace, built on the banks of the Thames in 1515-20, was transformed into a sumptuous royal residence at the end of the 17th century by the

famous architect Christopher Wren. The palace now houses paintings of the most famous Italian artists of the time, including Mantegna and Giorgione.

25 bottom A group of swans on the calm waters of the Thames below Windsor Castle, which was begun around the year 1070 by William the Conqueror. The castle, constructed on a natural terrace that overlooks the river, was rebuilt and beautified in the following centuries.

The girl had a curious personality: she loved to weave garlands along the banks of the Thames and saw white rabbits with pink eyes pop out of the grass and run past her.

Reading, the only industrial city on the upper and middle sections of the Thames, will always be known as the place where Oscar Wilde was imprisoned for homosexual offenses, followed two years later by his accuser, who was found guilty of false testimony. Farther down the river, at Marlow, Shelley found refuge for his tormented soul, while his wife Mary crafted her famous novel *Frankenstein* piece by piece and page by page.

Before Reading the bed of the Thames narrows as it passes through the Goring gorge, amidst the Chiltern Hills and the Berkshire Downs, an area rich in natural springs. The river is now in the London basin and flows slowly eastward in wide meanders through what in the past was a broad marshy valley.

Here the pastoral and agricultural Thames changes aspect and social class, becoming an aristocratic river. The members of the Royal Family and the leading exponents of the country's military, political and religious classes chose this area to build their sumptuous

residences, far from the overpopulated and unhealthy capital. The massive crenellated walls of Windsor Castle dominate the Thames from a natural rise. A huge park surrounds the edifice, which was founded by William the Conqueror in the later part of the 11th century and was remodeled and beautified in the following centuries. It is still the official residence of the royal family. Hampton Court, on the other hand, was turned into a museum. No expense was spared by Cardinal Wolsey, one of the wealthiest people in England, in the construction of this building in 1525, which was donated to Henry VIII a few years later. At the end of the 17th century it was completely rebuilt by the famous architect Christopher Wren, an extremely cultured person and the leading figure in the rebuilding of London after the disastrous fire of 1666.

Richmond, at the gates of London, was chosen as the residence of the Plantagenets, a dynasty that laid the foundation for the political development of the country. But it is between Hampton Court and Windsor that the weight of history makes itself felt even more. Two famous members of this family were Richard Lion-Heart and King John.

26-27 The profile of the Houses of Parliament, with their marked Gothic or Elizabethan style, dominates London's West End, which lies along the left bank of the Thames.

27 top This satellite view of the Thames winding through London, clearly shows the large areas of greenery or parks in the heart of the

city. Another characteristic feature of the city that can be seen in a wide bend in the river (at right), are the old East End docks.

27 center St. Paul's Cathedral (at left), whose construction drew inspiration from the classical Palladian style, is one of the most impressive buildings in London.

27 bottom The Houses of Parliament, Westminster Hall and Big Ben are reflected majestically in the waters of the Thames. Westminster Bridge, one of the 27 that cross the river, connects the heart of London and the densely populated quarters that lie along the river's south bank.

THE THAMES

The latter was forced by the English barons to sign the Magna Carta at Runnymede in 1215, in the setting of the open fields that border the southern bank of the Thames: for the first time in Europe, the dogma of royal absolutism was challenged and checked.

Several centuries earlier, the Saxons had crowned their bellicose kings at Kingston. The lock at Teddington, a short distance away, marks the beginning of the tidal part of the Thames, its estuary; this is 87 miles (140 km) long and its water level rises 23 ft (7 m) at high tide. But the tides can be even higher and may have devastating consequences. In 1953 London was flooded by the Thames; hundreds of people died and the damage was inestimable. In order to protect the city from any such exceptional events in the future, in 1982 a 60-ft (18-m) high mobile barrier was placed in the river at Woolwich, about 31 miles (50 km) from the the estuary.

The Thames crosses Greater London in a stone and cement bed. Here it is crossed by 27 bridges as well as by several railway and road tunnels. Famous buildings and monuments line the river: Westminster, the Tower, and Big Ben, symbols of a long-lived and illustrious civilization. But

28-29 The commercial traffic on the Thames, which the poet John Mansfield once called "a grand liquid thoroughfare," has now become almost negligible. Tower Bridge, a true wonder of Victorian engineering, is now one of the most popular tourist attractions in London.

28 bottom The Docklands zone, which was once the unloading point for the cargo transported from all the corners of the British Empire, is now the site of offices and residential areas.

29 top The futuristic Millennium Dome, on its Thames-side site at Greenwich, east of London, is the largest dome ever built. Opened on 31 December 1999 with the participation of the royal family, this structure has surface area of over 8.6 million sq.ft (80,000 sq. m), most of which is taken up by exhibition areas.

THE THAMES

29 bottom The two roofed footways that connect the central towers of the London's Tower Bridge were closed for a long period but were recently restored and opened to the public.

This famous bridge was built in 1894 and was provided with an ingenious mechanical lifting apparatus that made it possible to raise the roadways in only 90 seconds.

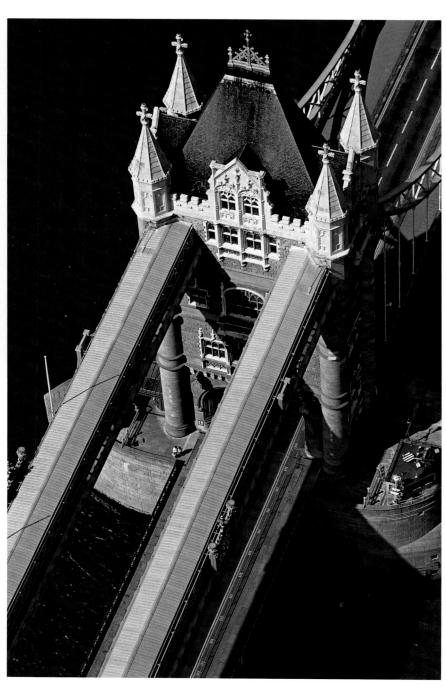

the "great road paved with water" and always filled with boats loaded with their cargo that went beyond the Tower Bridge, is now almost deserted. Most of the traffic has shifted toward Tilbury and the coastal ports, which can berth oceangoing ships. The old East End Docks, the grim setting for some of Dickens' novels and once the main clearing and sorting center of all the resources of the British Empire, have been converted into residential and office building zones. And the Thames, which was considered dead only a few decades ago, has taken on new life: the organic and industrial pollution that afflicted the river has been almost totally eliminated and the Atlantic salmon have begun to go upstream once again. At Gravesend the Thames loses itself in the embrace of the grey North Sea, "like the beginning of an endless waterway," as Joseph Conrad said.

30-31 The Thames Barrier, at Woolwich Reach, was conceived to protect London from floods caused by unusually high tides. The construction extends for about 1640 ft (500 m) across the Thames.

31 top and center top Endless horizons characterize the Thames estuary, broad expanses where the river meets the freezing waters of the North Sea: a primeval landscape, a vast expanse of liquid that Joseph Conrad described as the beginning of a "water highroad that leads to the most remote confines of the Earth." The tide goes up the river as far as Teddington, about 18.5 miles (30 km) upstream from London.

31 center bottom Many historic edifices mark the urban landscape of the London suburb of Greenwich, which lies along the winding course of the Thames. The most interesting sights include the National Maritime Museum and the old astronomical observatory, where Edmund Halley studied the comet that was named after him.

31 bottom The Old Royal Naval College, considered one of the masterpieces of English Baroque architecture, overlooks the Thames River. Built in the late 17th century to a design by Christopher Wren, this building is now the home of Greenwich University and Trinity College of Music.

THE THAMES

32 top Fed by many small affluents that descend from the Alps in the Grisons region of Switzerland, the Vorderrhein (Front Rhine) flows impetuously toward its junction with the waters of the Hinterrhein (Back Rhine). The true Rhine River begins a short distance downstream, at the town of Reichenau.

THE RHINE
THE ARTERY OF EUROPE

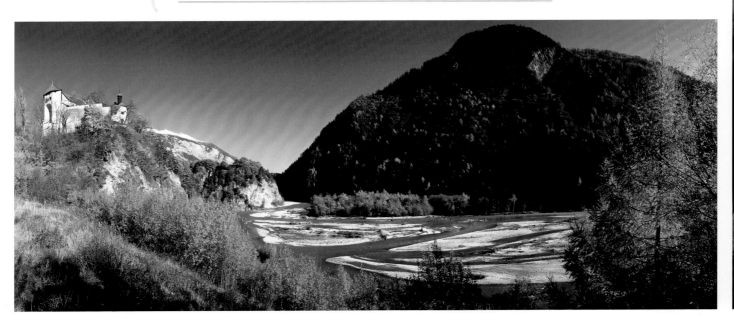

Every second, nine tons of goods pass through the docks of Rotterdam, at the mouth of the Rhine River, the largest port complex in the world: an amount three times that of Singapore and six times more than the cargo shipped through the docks of London. By itself, the dock used for mooring the new huge oil tankers, most of which come from the Persian Gulf, is as large as the entire port of Genoa. Besides petroleum, which is channeled directly to the refineries, the wharves of Rotterdam take in masses of wheat, produce, industrial products, metals, and building material. And above all, coal and iron ore, which are used to stoke the furnaces of the Ruhr region, the industrial heart of Germany. Rotterdam and all Holland owe their prosperity to the Rhine. Night and day, without a break, interminable rows of barges navigate down the river, which is the main artery of the European economy.

The Rhine is navigable as far as Basel, which amounts to 496 miles (800 km) into the interior, and a network of canals links it to all the other principal rivers in both Western and

Eastern Europe. The Seine, Rhône, Elbe, Saône, and the Danube, and all their affluents, therefore become part of the immense continental waterway that begins at the Dutch ports – a waterway that connects Bucharest with Frankfurt, Marseille and Bordeaux with Amsterdam, and Berlin with Paris. Grafted onto this colossal network of river and canal communications is the host of roads and railways that cross the Rhine valley in all directions, following the ancient trade routes used to transport tin, copper and amber. The same routes were used in the following centuries by the Christian monks, who crossed over the Alps to preach among the pagan peoples of the North.

From prehistoric times to the modern age the river has been a powerful catalyst of culture and civilization that has assimilated and metabolized inspiration and contributions from different and seemingly irreconcilable worlds. The Rhine valley has witnessed the rise of famous cities and cathedrals, as well as revolutions in politics, law, art and religion. The life and works of Marx, Rembrandt, Beethoven, Gutenberg, Heine and Erasmus are closely connected to the cosmopolitan and vital

32 bottom   At Rhazuns Castle in the Swiss Alps, the Back Rhine flows through an enchantingly beautiful landscape. This part of the river begins its course in the glaciers of the Rheinwaldhorn, at an altitude of about 9842 ft (3000 m), and then flows through a narrow gorge known as the Via Mala.

32-33   The snow-capped peaks of Piz Baduz, which rise 9842 ft (3000 m) meters above sea level, are mirrored in the placid waters of Lake Tuma: the sources of the Front Rhine, the west branch of the Rhine proper, are in this lake situated in the St. Gotthard Pass area of the Swiss-Italian border.

Rhine region. But the Rhine has two faces, or better, two opposing vocations: it both unites and divides. Quite often in the course of history the river was a frontier, a boundary to be conquered or to defend at any price. The first fortifications along the Rhine valley were erected almost 2,000 years ago by Julius Caesar to protect the eastern borders of the Roman Empire. Alans, Vandals, Burgundians, Franks and Huns fought for dominion of the riverbanks, which witnessed the fall of the Roman Empire and the rise of the Carolingian dynasties.

The history of the Rhine is a succession of invasions and bloody wars. It was a passageway for the Norman marauders, a battlefield where the Papacy and emperors fought one another, an object of the expansionist aims of the French and Prussians, and the symbolic and strategic backbone of the burgeoning nationalism in Europe. In the first decades of the 20th century the Rhine was transformed into an iron and cement trench: from Basel to Karlsruhe the Maginot Line and the Siegfried Line, filled with machine-gun nests and protected by mine fields, faced one another ominously. In Germany the Ruhr

region, the hub of the powerful war machine, became a gigantic furnace in the service of Hitler. The grim roar of the trip-hammers at Essen, where the Krupp steel plants mass-produced cannons and tanks, heralded the most frightful war that ever struck Europe. And the Rhine was its tragic protagonist. Thousands of tons of bombs turned the prosperous cities of the Ruhr into heaps of burning ruins; the roads and railways were systematically destroyed and the river was the only means of communication between northern and southern Germany. Only in early March 1945, after long and bitter battles, did the Allies succeed in breaking through the front on the Rhine at Remagen, below Bonn. The capture of this last bastion opened the way to Berlin, and Hitler's suicide two months later marked the end of World War Two. Bonn became the new capital of Germany and the Rhine, no longer a bitterly disputed frontier, resumed its role as an international mediator.

Almost as if to underscore its ambiguous destiny, the river consists of two merging torrents, the Vorderrhein and Hinterrhein, that is, the Front Rhine and Back Rhine, both of which rise in the Swiss Alps of the Grisons canton. The Back Rhine issues from the glaciers of the Adula massif, 7260 ft (2200 m) above sea level, and precipitates through a narrow gorge that the ancient Romans called the Via Mala. The second source comes from Lake Tuma, at the foot of the St. Gotthard Pass, and joins the Front Rhine near Reichenau, not far from the

660 ft to 1320 ft (200 m to 400 m) wide. A century of work was needed to adapt the river to the needs of humankind by shortening its course by about 62 miles (100 km). This does not mean that the Rhine has become innocuous. The major floods in 1993 and 1995, which overran vast regions of Germany and Holland, show how furious the harnessed river can become.

city of Chur. In the 43 miles (70 km) that separate it from Lake Constance, the Rhine has a gradient of about 4950 ft (1500 m); at the Austrian-Swiss border it is still an alpine river that flows rapidly among woods and green pastureland. Once out of Lake Constance it seems to calm down a bit and become a bit more 'mature,' as it were. But this is an illusion. A short distance farther on, at Schaffhausen, it becomes a bouncing youngster for the last time, rushing into a roaring falls amid whirls of foam and clouds of mist.

Now satisfied with having played this prank, it proceeds toward Basel, a large industrial center and Switzerland's only outlet to the sea. One of the leading figures of European humanism, Erasmus of Rotterdam, the author of *The Praise of Folly*, lived, worked and died here. At Basel the Rhine changes both direction and aspect: it turns sharply northward and becomes a huge navigable canal that flows in an artificial bed that is from

After Basel, the Rhine meanders through the large Rhine rift valley, which is embellished with the Black Forest and the low ridges of the Vosges Mts., crisscrossing the long stretch of the border between France and the German region of Baden. The rift valley, which resulted from the formation of the Alps 50 million years ago, accompanies the river for about 248 miles (400 km), up to the confluence with the Main. In its voyage through the plains of Alsace, the Rhine passes through Breisach, the ancient Roman city of Mons Brisiacus, and then arrives at Strasbourg, a major communications hub and flourishing commercial center. The spires of the Gothic Notre-Dame Cathedral dominate the profile of the Old Town, which has preserved its fascinating medieval atmosphere. Strasbourg, connected to the Marne, Rhône and Seine via a network of canals, is the home of the Central Rhine Commission, which establishes the rules of navigation along the river.

34 top Having passed through Lake Constance, which is a sort of regulatory basin, the Rhine flows toward the spectacular Schaffhausen Falls, near the Swiss-German frontier, where it plunges headlong for over 82 ft (25 m) amidst a blaze of mist and foam.

34 bottom Once past Chur, the Rhine enters a wide cultivated valley, becoming for a short stretch the border between Switzerland and Austria, and then gradually becomes less torrential as it flows toward Lake Constance.

34-35 The Rhine and a vast network of navigable canals are the basic factors in the commercial prosperity of Strasbourg, the capital of the French department of the Lower Rhine. The spires of Notre-Dame Cathedral dominate the historic center of the city.

35 bottom The village of Rheinau, situated in Switzerland near the border with Germany, lies along one of the large meanders formed by the Rhine downstream from the Schaffhausen Falls. On the island in the middle of the river is a Benedictine monastery.

THE RHINE

36-37 The steep valley formed by the Rhine when it crosses the massifs below Mainz is known in Germany as the legendary Heroes' Gorge, the landscape of which inspired Richard Wagner for some passages in his famous Ring cycle.

36 bottom left Situated on the Neckar River, a tributary of the Rhine, the city of Heidelberg is a major industrial and commercial center.

36 bottom right The sluices of a hydroelectric plant block the course of the Rhine at the Swiss city of Kaiseraugst, situated on the German border.

37 The castles and fortresses that rise up on the banks of the Rhine below Mainz, Germany, bear witness to the troubled medieval period in this region, when it was ruled by independent principalities.

At Karlsruhe the river becomes German and will remain so up to the beginning of the delta. This is the glorious middle section of the Rhine, which flows past a series of famous cities and landmarks. There is turreted Speyer, the triumph of Romanesque architecture: the cathedral, one of the largest Romanesque cathedrals in Europe, houses the tombs of five emperors. This town is followed by Heidelberg, on the Neckar River, with its famous university. Then there is Worms, where in the bitterly cold March of 1521, during the Diet of Worms attended by the princes of Germany, Emperor Charles V tried to persuade Luther to recant his religious ideas. Generated by the reaction against the corruption of the clergy and sale of indulgences, the Reformation shattered the religious unity of Europe forever; Luther's theses spread rapidly along the Rhine, from Holland to Switzerland, splitting the continent into two diametrically opposed camps.

At Mainz the Rhine receives the Main River, which by means of a major canal laid out in 1922 links it to the Danube. Its discharge is now considerable and constant all year long, thanks to a perfect combination of factors: during the summer the river takes in the water from the thawed Alpine snow, while the Neckar, Main, Moselle, Saar and other affluents of the middle section of the Rhine provide it with a copious supply of water during the winter, when the Atlantic rains are more abundant. The fame of Mainz is connected to Johann Gutenberg, the inventor of printing with movable type, made of metal and all of the same height. The first printed book in history, the so-called Gutenberg Bible or 42-line Bible, printed in two columns in red and black, was published in 1452 by the Gutenberg print shop. In the years following, German printers spread the new art throughout Europe, triggering one of the greatest cultural revolutions in the history of mankind.

THE RHINE

38-39 *The Burg Katz, or Cat's Castle, dominates the Rhine between Bingen and Koblenz, in Germany. Built in the 14th century, destroyed by the French in 1806 and then rebuilt, the fortress is now a popular tourist attraction.*

39 top *The Rheinstein castle, which was rebuilt in the 19th century, rises*

up over the hills that surround the so-called Heroes' Gorge of the Rhine, the valley that cuts through the Taunus mountains for 18 miles (30 km).

39 center *The castle of Stahleck, situated upstream from Koblenz, exudes a romantic atmosphere. Many of the Rhine castles have been converted into hotels, restaurants and museums.*

39 bottom *Pfalzgrafenstein, the fortress of Pfalz with a curious pentagonal shape, is one of the most fascinating edifices in the so-called Heroes' Gorge. Its position on an islet right in the middle of the Rhine made it easy for the local lord to exact tolls on those who used the river at this point.*

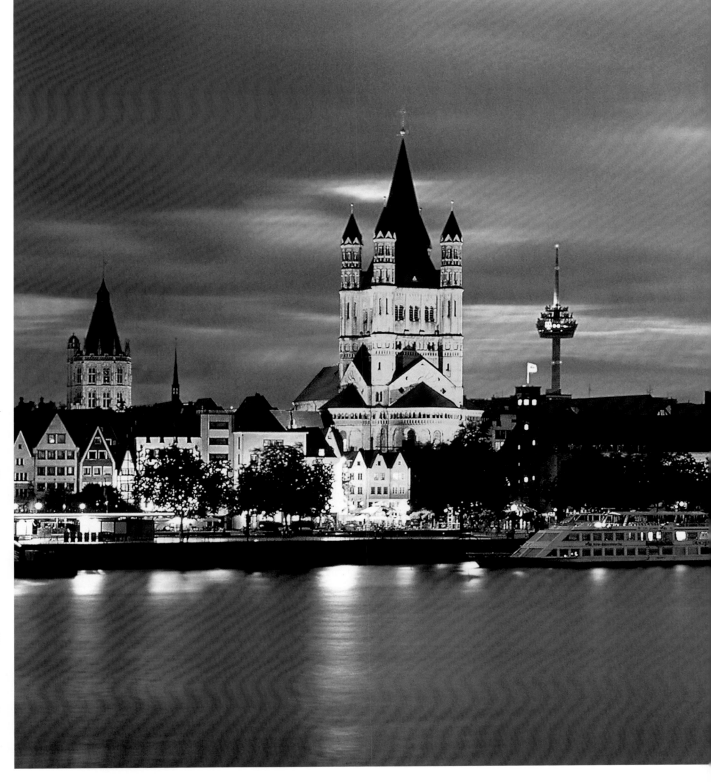

40-41 St. Peter's Cathedral is mirrored in the placid waters of the Rhine at Cologne, a lively river port and one of the most distinguished cities in western Germany. It took more than six centuries to build this colossal edifice, which was finally finished in 1880.

40 bottom Strategically situated at the junction of the Rhine and Moselle rivers, Koblenz is a leading industrial and commercial city. It was founded by the ancient Romans in 9 BC as a defensive outpost against the Germanic tribes but became prestigious and important only in the following centuries.

41 Mainz, the capital of the Rhine Palatinate, owes its prosperity to its enviable geographic position. Situated at the junction of the Rhine and Main rivers, Mainz is known for its prestigious cultural institutes and above all for the Printing Museum, dedicated to the work of Johann Gutenberg.

THE RHINE

History and legend interweave in the 34 miles (55 km) of the Heroes' Gorge, which is dotted with castles with evocative names: Burg Katz, Burg Maus, Rheinfels, Sterrenberg, Mauseturm, Drachenfels, and the disturbing polygonal fortress of Pfalz built on a islet in the middle of the Rhine. Lastly, there is Koblenz, at the confluence of the Moselle, the land of excellent wines thanks to the mild climate in this stretch of the valley, a sun-kissed area protected from the north winds by the surrounding mountains. Passing through a hilly region, the river reaches Bonn, the birthplace of Beethoven, and then Cologne. St. Peter's Cathedral, begun in 1248 and completed only in 1880, was miraculously spared by the Second World War bombardments, which razed one-third of the city to the ground.

From Cologne to the Dutch-German border the Rhine flows past a series of large cities and industrial centers. Leverkusen, Düsseldorf, Duisburg, Essen and Dortmund are really a single metropolis, one of the largest urban agglomerates

Once past Mainz, the Rhine faces the barrier of the Taunus range and the Rhenish Slate Mountains: at Binger Loch, instead of going around the obstacle, the river heads right for it, cutting its way through cliffs and slopes covered with woods and vineyards. This is the so-called Heroes' Gorge, the legendary land of the Nibelungen and of Siegfried, dragons and treasures that have been lost in depths of the river forever: the mythical hoard of gold of the Rhine, which inspired the first opera of Richard Wagner's Ring cycle, *Das Rheingold*. The Romantic movement, in search of a soul and a mythical identity, repopulated the gorges of the Rhine with supernatural beings who lived in the water and rocks: Lorelei, the siren who lures men to perdition and death, appears in poetry only in the early 19th century. Perhaps it was the echo that resounds on the rock faces of Lorelei, overlooking the Rhine from a height of 430 ft (130 m), which inspired the poem by Heine about the fatal girl.

in the world. In this section the river traffic becomes more intense, as the Ruhr receives raw material and gives back finished products at a frenetic pace. For decades, an unbelievable amount of pollutant material was dumped into the Rhine, changing the river into a boundless open-air sewer. Fortunately, in the last twenty years things have changed. The international Central Rhine Commission, founded in 1950 to protect the river, has enjoyed its first decisive success: after half a century of justified absence, the salmon have begun to reappear in the river together with other species that had not lived in the Rhine for many years.

After leaving the Ruhr region, the Rhine moves toward Holland. At Arnheim it splits into two distributaries, the Lek and the Waal, the latter of which receives the waters of the Maas. Silently, with aristocratic dignity, it then disappears in the vastness of the North Sea.

42-43 A characteristic feature of the landscape of Kinderdijk, near Rotterdam, are the rows of windmills. When it flows into the vast plains of the Netherlands the Rhine splits up into several branches and canals, taking in the waters of the Meuse River in a land that has been greatly modified by centuries of human labor.

43 top Futuristic architecture characterizes the modern city of Rotterdam, built in keeping with the most advanced town planning criteria. The city port, which extends around the mouth of the Rhine for dozens of miles, is now the largest in the world both in size and in the quantity of cargo handled.

43 center Delftshaven, the only remaining part of old Rotterdam, has become a true open-air museum surrounded by vast industrial zones. Standing out among the many historic buildings along the Voorhaven is the Oudekerk, the church frequented by the Pilgrims before they set off for the New World.

43 bottom Leiden, on the Old Rhine, has for centuries been the cultural and intellectual hub of the Netherlands. Its university, founded by William of Orange in 1575, is world-famous, as are the Lakenhal Museum and the National Ethnology Museum, which houses many rare and priceless archeological artifacts.

THE RHINE

44-45 and 44 bottom These photographs clearly show the vastness of the delta of the Volga River, which, when it empties into the Caspian Sea, breaks up into a multitude of canals and radiates out over an area of 7725 sq. miles (20,000 sq. km). During the spring floods, which raise the level of the water from 6.5 to 16.5 ft (2 to 5 m), the apearance of the delta undergoes a drastic change, as can be seen in the photo at right: the sandy islands that formed after the recent lowering of the water level of the Caspian Sea, are submerged.

45 An aerial views of the entire course of the Volga River, from its source in the Valdaï hills to its mouth in the Caspian Sea. In this photograph one can easily spot the large reservoirs of Volgograd and Kuybyshev; in the lower left-hand part are Cimljansk Lake and the Don River.

Nizhniy Novgorod

Kazan

Samara

Saratov

Volgograd
(Tsaritsyn)

Astrakhan

THE VOLGA

THE SOUL OF RUSSIA

This river rises in the Valdaï Hills, about 186 miles (300 km) as the crow flies from the Gulf of Finland. Enveloping Russia in a colossal embrace, the Volga crosses forests, steppes and deserts until it reaches the shores of the Caspian Sea. For the Russians it is the Mother Volga, the river around which the identity of the nation rose up and was consolidated. Only when Ivan the Terrible managed to wrest the Volga territory from the Tatar hordes by conquering the Mongol strongholds of Kazan and Astrakhan, was Russia truly a united nation. And the river, which is an ethnic and cultural boundary between Europe and Asia, was the base of the Cossack conquest of Siberia in the name of the czar. The banks of the middle and lower Volga were also the center of the peasant rebellions led by Stenka Razin in 1669-70 and by Pugachev in 1773-74. In the spring of 1918, Samara and Simbirsk, on the middle section of the river, witnessed the rise of the first pockets of resistance against Bolshevik power: revolutionaries and counter-revolutionaries waged a ruthless war to conquer the cities along the Volga. The bloody battles for control of Tsaritsyn underscored the skills and determination of one of the toughest and most callous Soviet leaders, in whose honor the city was later named: Stalingrad. And it was here that the Volga proved to be an insuperable barrier for Hitler's divisions. The defeat of the Germans marked a turning point in the Second World War and in the history of Europe.

The backbone of Russia, since the early Middle Ages the Volga has played the role of communications route between the northern and southern regions of the country. The river and its tributaries form a gigantic longitudinal axis that connects highly different regions, from the northern forests to the arid lands of the Caspian Sea. The climatic and environmental differences of these regions are reflected in their productive diversity, which from the outset has influenced the river traffic: petroleum and industrial products have been added to merchandise such as lumber, wheat, wool and cotton. Thanks to the geological features of its basin, the Volga is navigable from its mouth almost to the headstreams. Despite this, its economic potential was greatly penalized by the fact the river issues into an inland sea that is isolated from the major modern trade routes.

The first attempts at linking the river with the Baltic Sea and St. Petersburg date from the time of the czars, but it was only in the 1930s that the Volga was drastically transformed. The new Soviet regime under Stalin launched a colossal project, the so-called Five Seas system, which was intended to connect the Volga, by means of a series of navigable canals, to the main rivers in Russian and then to the Baltic Sea, Black Sea, White Sea, Sea of Azov and Caspian Sea. At the same time, a chain of huge artificial basins would provide the Soviet Union with the hydroelectric power needed for its five-year plans of industrialization and would furnish enough water to irrigate vast stretches of unproductive land. After fifty years of continuous labor, the course of the Volga was completely changed. However, the hoped-for results did not materialize. The lakes created by the locks and dams in the uniform Samartian plain are rather shallow and too large; consequently, the power furnished by the dam turbines was much less than what had been foreseen and enormous areas of cultivable land were flooded. The level of the Caspian Sea, which is no longer constantly fed by the Volga River, has decreased by 82 ft (25 m). Furthermore, the dams blocked the migration of the sturgeon, which could not reach their reproduction habitats; their population was therefore drastically reduced, as was the production of the caviar made from the eggs of this fish.

The present-day Volga, controlled by numerous dams and at the service of the Russian nation, is no longer the wild river described by Chekhov and Gorki, both of whom traveled on its

46-47 The island of Kizhi on Lake Onega has been converted into an open-air museum that offers an overall view of Russian history. A series of canals links the lake with the Volga and allows for river navigation toward the Baltic Sea and the White Sea.

46 *bottom In this village in the region northeast of Moscow, life has retained its centuries-old rhythm. Already at its source the Volga is a full-fledged river that makes its way into the immensity of the Sarmatian plain.*

47 *The old wooden buildings, windmills and scenes of everyday life on the island of Kizhi, in Lake Onega, inevitably lead one to think of Russian rural life in the past. In reality, for some time now the Lake Onega region has been part of the* major commercial activities centered around the Volga River. The gigantic works carried out in the 1930s and in the postwar period created a system of navigable waterways that link the Black Sea with the Baltic Sea and the White Sea with the Caspian.

THE VOLGA

waters, the former during his honeymoon and the latter working in the gallery of a boat in search of that humble, desperate and destitute Russia so vividly portrayed in his novels. A friend of Gorki in the adventurous years he spent at Kazan was Feodor Chaliapin, who before becoming one of the world's foremost operatic stars of all times, sang in church choirs. This great bass spread the song of the Volga boatman throughout the world; it was originally the song of the landless, poverty-stricken peasants, the *burlaki*, who earned their living by pulling the boats up the river with ropes. The painter Ilya Repin immortalized their daily fatigue in his canvas *Volga Boatmen*: behind the row of tattered, suffering men, the blue and gold waters of the Volga seem to melt into the sky.

Art, history, politics and all the misery and dreams of Russia are an integral part of the Volga. As if it were conscious of such an oppressive destiny, the river is already in an adult stage when it rises at an altitude of only 890 ft (270 m) above sea level. A short distance after its sources it has all the earmarks of a full-fledged plains river, wide and deep enough to allow small boats to navigate in it. At Tver (Kalinin), before winding into the Ivankovo reservoir, it is 660 ft (200 m) wide. An 80-mile (128-km) canal built in 1937 links it to Moscow. A short distance farther on the river flows into the lake at Rybinsk; other canals radiate toward the Northern Dvina and the Onega and Ladoga lakes, which in turn communicate with the White Sea and the Gulf of Finland. From the confluence with the Oka River, near Nizhny Novgorod, up to Volgograd the course of the Volga is interrupted by a series of dams: the Kama River, arriving from the Ural Mts., flows into the Volga in the immense Kuybyshev Reservoir, which has a surface area of 2580 sq. miles (6450 sq. km), that is, twelve times larger than Lake Constance. At Saratov the last affluents abandon the Volga and tall trees give way to the faceless expanse of the steppe. The connection with the Don River, realized after World War Two, completes a navigable system that is 9300 miles (15,000 km) long, running from one end of Russia to the other and linking Archangel and the ports of the Arctic Sea with Odessa, St. Petersburg and Astrakhan.

The first cities along the Volga rose up as trade centers that benefited from both the inland and transverse traffic between Asia and Europe. It was the merchants who built the numerous churches at Yaroslavl with their characteristic onion domes. For centuries Yaroslavl, Uglich and Kostroma, founded at the beginning of the 12th century, played a leading cultural and economic role in the region between the upper section of the Volga and the Oka River, the nucleus of old Grand Duchy of Muscovy. Uglich was the base from which Ivan the Terrible launched the series of attacks that finally eliminated the power of the Golden Horde forever. In the Kremlin of Uglich, Boris Godunov assassinated Ivan's young son in the 1590s, thus initiating the dramatic power struggle that afflicted Russia up to the ascent of the Romanov dynasty. And precisely at Kostroma, Godunov's hometown, Michael Romanov was crowned in 1613.

Farther down the river, where the Oka flows into the Volga, is Nizhny Novgorod, the birthplace of Maxim Gorki. However, it was at Kazan that this author wrote *My Universities* before attempting to commit suicide by shooting himself in the chest.

48-49 The profiles of the churches in Uglich stand out in the snow-clad terrain surrounding this city, which was founded along the Volga in 937. One of these churches is dedicated to the memory of Dimitri, the son of Ivan the Terrible and the victim of a dynastic power struggle that paved the way for Boris Godunov's ascension to the throne.

49 bottom This fisherman is armed with a large auger that he will use to bore a hole in the ice covering the Volga northwest of Moscow; he will then lower his fishing line into the freezing river. In the northern regions the river may freeze over for long periods, even as much as 200 days.

THE VOLGA

50-51 *A Russian Orthodox church towers over the office buildings and harbor facilities situated at the confluence of the Volga and Oka rivers, in the Gorki region. Industrial pollution is posing a serious threat to the very survival of the fish species that live in the Volga.*

50 bottom *The monastery of Makarev emerges like an apparition from the waters of the Volga, downstream from the city of Gorki. The sincere faith of the Russian people is attested by the profusion of religious buildings and icons, the sacred images that were worshipped by families in their homes.*

51 *Kazan, the ancient capital of the Golden Horde, still has traces of its past. In this photograph we can see the walls of the Kremlin ('fortress' in Russian) and the new mosque, which was built thanks to the contribution of Saudi Arabia to replace the one destroyed by Ivan the Terrible in 1552.*

THE VOLGA

Kazan, the capital of the Tatar Republic, marks the northern border of former Islamic dominion. Batu Khan, a descendant of Jenghiz Khan, turned this city into one of the nerve centers of the Mongol empire. The Tatars remained in Kazan even after the Russians conquered it and still make up the majority of the population. Tolstoy studied Philosophy and Oriental languages in this cosmopolitan atmosphere. Forty years later, at the same university, a certain Vadimir Ulyanov, better known as Lenin, was accused of subversive activity and expelled from the law school. Kazan, Kuybyshev (Samara), Saratov, Togliatti (Stavropol until 1964) and Ulyanovsk (formerly Simbirsk but renamed for Lenin as he was born there) are now important agricultural and industrial centers.

Peace and newfound liberty now reign along the Volga River. But a tragic, bloody trace of the past still remains at

Volgograd: the grim ruins of a factory destroyed by bombardments and riddled by machine-gun bullets remind us that this city was once called Stalingrad. Hitler wanted to capture the city at all costs, and Stalin told his soldiers that they had to resist to the last man. For five months Stalingrad, which had become a heap of rubble, was the theater of bitter house-to-house fighting. The Germans surrendered in February 1943, and once again the Volga had saved Russia.

After Volgograd the river proceeds to the petroleum transportation port of Astrakhan and the Caspian basin, which lies 99 ft (30 m) below sea level. The Volga delta, a maze of waterways and canals that spread out for 124 miles (200 km), is an oasis throbbing with life. Beyond the shores of the river there is the desert. Much like a mirage, the horizon fades away toward the arid plains of Central Asia.

THE SEINE

THE CRADLE OF ART

This river rises in Paris. Not in the center of town and not even in the outskirts, but about 124 miles (200 km) as the crow flies from the boundaries of the French capital, in the Langres Plateau, among the soft hills of Burgundy.

The small wooded area that surrounds the source of the Seine was purchased in the 19th century by the municipality of Paris, and since that time it been under the city's

jurisdiction. This was a right and proper homage, because the prosperity and fortune of the French capital is mainly due to the river, and the Seine and Paris are inseparable.

Yet the Seine is certainly not the most important river in France, as both the Loire and Rhône are longer, nor does it occupy a central position that would make it the political and commercial hub of the country. Again, other cities such as Tours, Lyons and Orléans have surpassed Paris in wealth and prestige over the centuries. Although it has been relegated into obscurity several times, Paris has always managed to rise up again, becoming greater, more beautiful and more luminous each time. Paris is the very heart of France, the symbol of universality and excellence in art and culture, and

famous for the simple *joie de vivre* of its citizens. The great author Honoré de Balzac called it a "sublime vessel loaded with intelligence," a ship solidly anchored to the two banks of the river the passes through it.

The preeminence of Paris is due to its geographic position in the middle of the Seine basin. Like the bottom of a funnel, the city is the natural focal point of all the communication routes in the region. The Île-de-France plain, bounded by almost imperceptible hills, is in fact easily accessible from all corners of France. This central role was augmented by the system of canals that connect the Seine and the ports of the English Channel with the other French rivers and with the Rhine, the access to the important industrial areas of Belgium and Germany. And Paris itself rose up on the water: what the ancient Romans called the *oppidum Parisiorum*, the Celtic city of the Parisii, stood on the Île de la Cité, now occupied by the towering presence of Notre-Dame Cathedral. The river-based origin of the city is demonstrated by certain aspects of the town plan, which is laid out in some stretches along the old course of the river. The name of the Marais district is connected to the marshes that once covered the area, and Montmartre was one of the characteristic rises that bordered the Seine. The name of the Seine is also of Celtic origin, as it derives from the word *squan*, "sinuous" and "serpentine," which is a perfect description, since the river is 480 miles (775 km) long, but as the crow flies it is a little more than half that length from its sources to the sea. Its meandering course, especially in the Paris basin, is like a sinuous wave that repeats itself with perfection. The same word *squan* became Sequana, who was a goddess for the Gauls and whom the Romans assimilated in their mythology, even building a temple in her honor at the river source.

According to legend, the desperate tears the nymph Sequana shed while being chased by a lustful satyr were transformed into a river.

52 top Commissioned by
Napoleon III, the sculpure that
marks the source of the Seine
reminds one of the statue of the
Roman goddess Sequana.

52 bottom The square bell
towers of Notre-Dame
Cathedral rise up majestically
over Île de la Cité, the heart of
medieval Paris.

52-53 The Eiffel Tower,
considered one of the most
audacious achievements of 19th-
century engineering and the symbol
of Paris, was planned by adopting
the already tried and tested system
used for bridge piers. About 80,000
tons of iron were used in the
structure, which was finished on
31 March 1889.

53 bottom The enormous Louvre
Museum complex on the right bank
of the Seine occupies a surface area
of about 50 acres (20 hectares)
and was initially used as the
residence of the kings of France.
Only in 1793, following a
deliberation of the Constituent
Assembly, was it converted into a
museum and opened to the public.
(The image captures the acrobatic
Patrouille de France flying over the
Louvre.)

From the interior of a rock-cut grotto, a statue of the divine girl watches over the transparent spring from which the Seine begins its run toward the valley at an altitude of only 1550 ft (470 m). About 9.5 miles (15 km) from here, on Mt. Auxois, Julius Caesar's legions defeated Vercingetorix in the Battle of Alesia in 52 BC, thus establishing a Roman hegemony over Gaul that lasted five centuries.

Although they were divided by tribal discord, the Celtic populations that lived in the Seine basin had a developed and

well-organized society. Trade with the Mediterranean countries flourished, as is demonstrated by archaeological finds. The so-called Vix Vase, found near Chatîllon where the Seine receives the Douix and becomes wide enough to justify the erection of bridge, is almost certainly of Greek origin. This krater made of decorated bronze, over 5 ft (1.5 m) high and weighing 457 lbs (208 kg), is 2600 years old. How it ended up in the forests of northern France as part of the grave goods of a Gallic princess is still a mystery, one of the many the Seine jealously keeps.

THE SEINE

54 top The Alexander III bridge, erected in 1900 to celebrate the International Exposition and decorated with seventeen large piers surmounted by allegorical statues, represents the triumph of Belle Époque

decorative art. In the background is the dome of the Hôtel des Invalides.

54 bottom The Seine and Notre-Dame Cathedral represent the quintessence of Paris. Pope Alexander

III laid the first foundation stone of this gigantic edifice, which took 170 years to finish, with the contribution of thousands of artisans and workers. The basilica is 426.5 ft (130 m) long and 230 ft (70 m) high.

54-55 The Pont Neuf, one of the oldest bridges in Paris, was finished in 1604 during the reign of Henry IV. Consisting of two sections, it connects the banks of the Seine with the tip of Île de la Cité.

THE SEINE

56 top One of the typical bâteaux-mouches proceeds down the placid waters of the Seine toward the Pont Neuf, in the heart of Paris. Nowadays these boats are used only for water-borne tours of the city, but in the past they transported over 25 million people a year.

56 center Originally a camp for Celtic fishermen on the banks of the Île de la Cité, Paris is now one of the largest and most beautiful cities in the world. On the Île des Cygnes, seen in the middle of this photograph, is a replica of the Statue of Liberty.

56 bottom Overlooking the Seine, the impressive Conciergerie dominates the western section of the Île de la Cité. An example of 14th-century French architecture, the Conciergerie became notorious as a prison during the French Revolution.

56-57 The spectacular profile of Notre-Dame stands out against the Parisian sky, illuminated by the sunset. In the interior of the basilica are important sacred relics, and also the mantle worn by Napoleon during his coronation.

58-59 *Château Gaillard, at Les Andelys, overlooks the valley sculpted by the Seine among the rocky lowlands of Normandy.*

58 bottom left and right *The basin of the Seine, bounded by low hills and characterized by slight gradients, is all that remains of a sea gulf that in remote times extended as far as the outskirts of present-day Paris. In its lower stretch through the plains of Normandy, the river is broad and flows quietly, proceeding slowly toward its mouth in the North Sea. Gigantic meanders alternate with short straight stretches in open terrain that has been altered and shaped by centuries of labor on the part of Man.*

59 *Continuous barge traffic goes down the Seine from the estuary as far as Bar-sur-Seine, which is inland at a distance of 350 miles (560 km). Thanks to its slight gradient and regular water intake, the river is easy to navigate.*

THE SEINE

Having passed through Burgundy, the Seine moves toward the ancient city of Troyes, thus entering the Champagne region, home of the most famous wine in the world. It seems that the secret of champagne production, which is based on a particular method of natural fermentation and complex processing, was discovered in the 17th century by the monk Dom Pérignon. After Troyes, the Seine, now channeled and curbed by a series of locks, becomes navigable for commercial traffic. Flowing through open, undulating countryside, the river arrives at the confluence with the Yonne. At Fontainebleau the regular alternation of woods and farm fields gives way to much more aristocratic geometric patterns. Some of the leading European artists and architects of the time, from Benvenuto Cellini to Vignola and Rosso

Until then his ancestors had been content to go up the Seine every so often in their *drakar* craft to make violent raids on the coastal towns. Rollo, on the other hand, worked at consolidating his reign; he reclaimed long stretches of the lower course of the Seine, built embankments against flooding, and had the riverbed dredged to make it navigable as far as the port of Rouen.

The Seine has a regular water intake: rainfall is constant on the entire surface of the basin but is almost never excessive. In fact, high water levels are rather rare, at least compared to the average of the other European rivers, partly because of the slight gradient of the current. At Paris, 226 miles (365 km) from the English Channel, its course is only 82 ft (25 m) above sea level. From Saint-Germain-en-Laye to

Fiorentino, took part in the construction of the majestic Fontainebleau palace, built in 1528 for King Francis I. The best experiences of the Italian and French Renaissance merged in the realization of the palace, which Vasari considered the glorious revival of a second Rome. In the following years the face of Paris changed and it became a true metropolis: the Louvre, Jardin de Plantes, Luxembourg Palace and many other monumental edifices date from that golden age in French history.

The banks of the Seine were also laid out anew and some of its affluents were made navigable. However, the first human changes on the river had been effected many centuries earlier. Already in the year 911 the Viking ruler Rollo grasped the importance of the river as a trade route to the interior.

the outskirts of Paris the Seine accentuates its winding flow, describing huge meanders in the vast plain that extends as far as the coast of the Channel. In this limestone lowland that was once covered with seawater, the erosive action of the river has cut a bed that is at times deep and embanked. In the areas where the riverbanks are steeper there are fortresses and castles, such as at Les Andelys, which is dominated by the ruins of Château Gaillard, built by Richard Lion-Heart to defend Rouen, the most anglophile French city. It was in fact at Rouen, before a court at the mercy of the English, that Joan of Arc was condemned to be burned at the stake, a form of torture used for witches and heretics. Her ashes were then cast into the Seine.

THE SEINE

Rouen is the destination of ocean-going ships, at once a sea and river port: the tides, which occur four times a day, determine the traffic on the river. Thousands of barges move incessantly in the estuary and, by means of a system of inland waterways that are navigable for 5000 miles (8000 km), they distribute all kinds of goods to the farthest corners of France. The boatmen are bonded by a strong sense of solidarity. The barge is both a house and a work tool; all family life is lived on board, and often the work is handed down from father to son. Conflans-Sainte-Honorine, at the junction of the Seine and the Oise, is the capital of these river nomads. Besides workshops and ship repair yards, this locality has cafés, restaurants, markets, and even a floating church and hospital.

Under the high, pale sky of Normandy the Seine leaves behind the spires of the Rouen Cathedral, only to meet the Gothic style again at the splendid church of Notre-Dame in Caudebec-en-Caux. In 1858 at Honfleur, the old port that was abandoned in favor of the active Le Havre, the artists Boudin and Monet began to represent the effects of light in their oil paintings. Impressionism was thus born at the point where the Seine dies in the grey waters of the northern seas.

60 top Its depth of up to 33 ft (10 m) means that ocean-going ships can navigate down the Seine as far as the river port of Rouen, which lies about 75 miles (120 km) from the sea. Pilotage is obligatory for all vessels over 150 ft (45 m) long.

60 bottom Enthusiastic spectators greet the passage of this sailboat participating in a commemorative regatta on the Seine as it passes through Normandy. The first people to grasp the importance of the river as a means of penetrating the interior were the Vikings, who were here over ten centuries ago.

60-61 Rouen, the capital of the Seine-Maritime department and a busy river port on the estuary of the Seine, takes in from 3500 to 4000 cargo ships every year. The city, known as the site of Joan of Arc's martyrdom, boasts one of the most beautiful Gothic cathedrals in France.

61 bottom The Normandy Bridge, which connects the two banks of the Seine near its mouth, is 1.3 miles (2.1 km) long and has a central span measuring over 2624 ft (800 m). Opened in 1995, it was built with state-of-the-art technology and is able to withstand winds of 185 mph (300 km).

THE LOIRE

ARISTOCRATIC BEAUTY

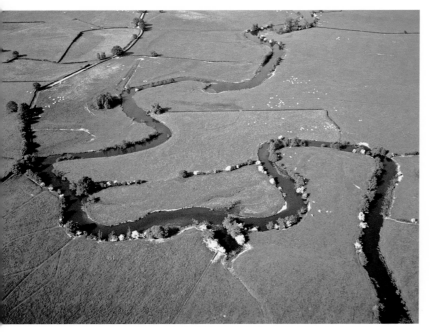

The wide arc described by the Loire River, from the Cévennes Mts. to the Atlantic coast, looks as if it had set out to divide France in two. In the Middle Ages, during the Hundred Years' War (1337-1453), the river was indeed an inland frontier: the English, allied with the Burgundians, dominated the north of France and the Seine delta, while to the south the French monarchy prepared to drive out the invaders and rebuild national unity. Since Paris was abandoned, the nerve center of the kingdom shifted to the shores of the Loire and remained there even after the English were defeated, up to the rise of the Bourbon dynasty. For this entire period the destiny of France was decided in the labyrinthine interiors of the Loire châteaux, which were transformed into luxurious residences and symbols of royal power. Many centuries later, during the time of the Franco-Prussian War, the river became the last defensive line against the onslaught of Bismarck's troops. Then, at the beginning of the Second World War, the French Army tried to organize resistance to Nazi occupation by establishing a bridgehead along the fords of the Loire. In both cases these military actions failed. But General Patton, who was advancing toward the Rhine and the heart of Germany, used the swirling waters of the river to protect the southern flank of the Allied armies.

The great events of history that the Loire witnessed now seem remote to us, buried in the timeless tranquility of the French provinces. But the Loire has remained young and wild. In its 632-mile (1020-km) course it touches such important cities as Orléans, Angers, and Tours. Nantes, one of the most active port towns in France, lies on the river estuary, and canals link the Loire to the Seine, the Saône and the Rhône. And four nuclear power plants utilize its waters for cooling, which has alarmed environmentalists but is really nothing compared to the problems besetting the other great European rivers in this respect. There is no commercial traffic on the Loire and the large industrial areas are almost totally lacking there. It has very few dams and levees, and they are all located in the upper section of the river, checking its impetus.

The Loire River defies the norm: it is the only waterway in Western Europe that maintains its natural features from the source to the mouth. Up to the mid-20th century the seasonal farm workers had a stipulation in their contracts to the effect that they would not be obliged to eat salmon more than four times a week. Although they are not so abundant as they once were, the fish are still numerous and quite varied. Because of its beautiful natural scenery, art treasures and environmental qualities, in the year 2000 the Loire Valley was placed on the UNESCO World Heritage List.

The river rises at the foot of one of the volcanic peaks in the Ardèche department, which because of its typical conical

62 top After Orléans the Loire River, which in certain stretches becomes a sort of rapids, crosses fertile countryside where fruit and cereals are grown. The flour produced in large quantities by the Meung-sur-Loire mills was once transported along the river, giving rise to flourishing commerce.

62 bottom The Loire winds its way through the vast plains of central France amid incomparably beautiful natural scenery. There are very few artificial dams or sluices that regulate the course of the Loire, which is the only river in Europe that does not suffer from excessive economic and commercial exploitation.

62-63 The course of the Loire, which is broad and filled with sandbars that change their shape and position with every flood, wends its way among the fertile land in the Loire-et-Cher department. The uniformity of the landscape actually conceals an extremely rich and diverse historic and social reality.

64-65 *Near Nantes the Loire changes its appearance, shedding its guise of a wild, uncontaminated river. After its junction with the Erdre, its last affluent, it gradually widens, forming a long estuary that extends up to St.-Nazaire, where it then empties into the Atlantic Ocean.*

64 bottom *The stetch between Orléans and Tours is one of the most fascinating in the Loire Valley. Because of its striking beauty and history, and above all for its exceptional art treasures, in 2000 UNESCO placed the entire region on the World Heritage List.*

65 top *The area traversed by the Loire near St.-Florent-le-Vieil is saturated with history: in March 1793 it was the venue of the beginning of the bloody civil war between the Catholic farmers of the Vendée and the new French Republic created by the French Revolution.*

65 bottom *Up to the early 20th century the transportation of goods and passengers on the Loire was used sailboats or steamboats, which traveled incessantly between Nevers and Nantes. The rise of the railway system marked the rapid end of river transport.*

shape is called Gerbier de Jonc, or "Sheaf of Rushes." At a swift pace, the Loire flows downward, opening its way in a basalt bed among mountain pastures and the ruins of medieval fortresses. Its transparent and rushing waters reach Le Puy, a pilgrimage site known for its miraculous healing: indeed, it was a miracle that the imposing Romanesque cathedral built at the end of the 12th century escaped the anti-religious fury of the French Revolution. After Le Puy the scenery becomes less rugged; the hills are replaced by the humid Forez plain, which the river crosses by bouncing from one rapid to another. Little by little the Loire becomes wider and flows in a vast sandy bed, gradually growing mellow together with the surroundings, which become softer and softer and are now modeled by human hands. The buildings and churches pass almost inadvertently from the sober Romanesque style to soaring Gothic architecture, in a sort of ideal transition to the glories of the Renaissance.

Nevers, at the confluence with the Nièvre River, is known for its production of majolica: Luigi Gonzaga of Mantua, who was Duke of Nevers in 1565, introduced the sophisticated technique of glazed porcelain from Italy. A short distance farther on, the Loire receives a considerable amount of water from the Allier and proceeds toward Sancerre and La Charité. The 16th-century wars between Catholics and Protestants left massacres in their wake on these hills, which are now covered with vineyards and wrapped in thoughtful tranquility. In its huge bend northward the river touches the basin of the Seine, to which it is connected by means of the Briare canal.

The opulent, theatrical Loire, with its castles and courts, begins at Gien, keeping a low profile, as it were: the Gien manor is light years away from the luxury and frivolity of the Chambord and Chenonceaux châteaux, as well as from the military rigor of Sully, a few miles below. This latter was built at

66-67 During the Renaissance the part of the Loire River Valley between Orléans and Tours became the political focal point of France. Kings, nobles and leading court officials chose it as their new home, building their sumptuous and elegant residences along the riverside.

66 bottom Protected by its massive bastions and deep moats, the Sully-sur-Loire château is a perfect example of medieval military architecture. This fortress, which for four centuries belonged to the descendants of the Duc de Sully, is now the property of the Loiret department and is used as the venue of exhibitions and important cultural events open to the public.

67 top In the past the flooding of the Loire was devastating. In 1856 the heart of Tours was awash and the river invaded the surrounding countryside, creating a lake 25 miles (40 km) long.

67 center Built in the late 14th century in the vicinity of one of the rare fording points of the Loire, the Sully-sur-Loire château was the residence of the Duc de Sully, the powerful finance minister of King Henry IV.

67 bottom The town of Gien lies on the banks of the Loire, at the foot of the large château built in 1484 for Anne de Beaujeu, daughter of Louis XI. This rather austere edifice is now the home of the International Hunting Museum.

THE LOIRE

the behest of Anne de Beaujeu, the daughter of Louis XI, immediately after the feudal wars that led to the unification of France, when parsimony and sobriety were much appreciated virtues: only the rhythmic succession of the geometric decoration in black and red attenuates the austerity of this edifice.

The Loire unexpectedly becomes working-class before arriving at Orléans, at Châteauneuf, home of an interesting naval museum. The golden age of river traffic was achieved in the mid-19th century, when 10,000 vessels navigated along the Loire, but this period came to a sharp halt a few decades later with the arrival of the first railways. In any case, navigation was by no means simple, as the river has an unstable regimen in which furious floods alternate with periods of severe drought. At Tours in the summer of 1933 the water level was so low that one could go to the other shore on foot with no trouble at all. The Loire then arrives at Orléans, whose name is linked with the exploits of Joan of Arc, crossing a region covered with forests and moors dotted with ponds and rich in game. Hunting, which had become a refined game, was one of the favorite pastimes of the illustrious tenants in the so-called Garden of France.

From Blois to Angers the course of the river boasts a series of sumptuous castles and châteaux: from Charles VII to Francis I, all the kings of France had their residences on the middle section of the Loire. Built not for defensive purposes but for the sheer pleasure of living, the Loire châteaux are the symbol of an epoch. A multitude of famous architects, landscape gardeners and artists – mostly Italians – transformed the sad medieval fortresses into masterpieces of Renaissance art and architecture.

Chambord is located in the middle of an estate that is as large as Paris: 400 rooms, 365 windows, a forest of monumental

THE LOIRE

towers and chimneys – an undertaking, or act of folly, that kept 2000 workmen occupied for twenty years, from 1519 to 1539. Blois was the theater of intrigues and assassinations, and its octagonal spiral staircase may have been designed by Leonardo da Vinci. The Italian genius was the guest of King Francis I and spent the last three years of his life surrounded by the drab walls of Amboise, the château founded by Charles VIII in the late 1400s that for over a century was the seat of royal power. Then there is Chaumont, so massive and solemn. And Chenonceaux, stretching out over the placid waters of the Cher River and so magnificent in its frivolity: Henry II gave it as a present to his mistress, Diane de Poitiers, who had splendid gardens laid out around it. When the king died, his wife Catherine de' Medici finally got revenge on her rival, having her interned in the grim bastions of Chaumont.

Once past Tours, the Loire receives the Indre and Vienne rivers. There are more châteaux at Azay-le-Rideau, Langeaux, and Villandry, which are immersed in an idyllic setting of forests and streams. There is an aura of mystery about the slender towers of Ussé, which inspired Charles Perrault's fairy tale *Sleeping Beauty*. Leaving behind the cyclopean wall of the Angers fortress, the river proceeds toward Nantes. Before opening out into a wide estuary toward the Atlantic Ocean, the river takes in the Mayenne and Erdre, its last affluents. Then, with noble indifference, it offers itself to the sea.

68-69 Power and elegance are merged in the architecture of the Chambord château, the largest in the Loire Valley.

68 bottom left Château Amboise, built by Charles VIII in the late 1400s, was one of the favorite residences of the kings of France.

68 bottom right The walls of the castle of Angers were erected during the reign of Louis IX (St. Louis), at the beginning of the 13th century.

69 top The broad and majestic Loire washes the town of Saumur, which is dominated by the château that was once the residence of the powerful Plantagenets. During the Second World War Saumur was the theater of heroic resistance against the German invasion and occupation.

69 bottom A massive fortress that has been rebuilt and enlarged several times over the centuries towers over the picturesque town of Chinon, on the banks of the Vienne, a tributary of the Loire.

70-71 Magnificent woods and gardens surround Chenonceaux, which was built by the architects of the Tours school and donated in 1547 by King Henry II to his mistress Diane de Poitiers. A 200-ft (60-m) roofed bridge with five arches crosses over the transparent waters of the Cher, which flows into the Loire.

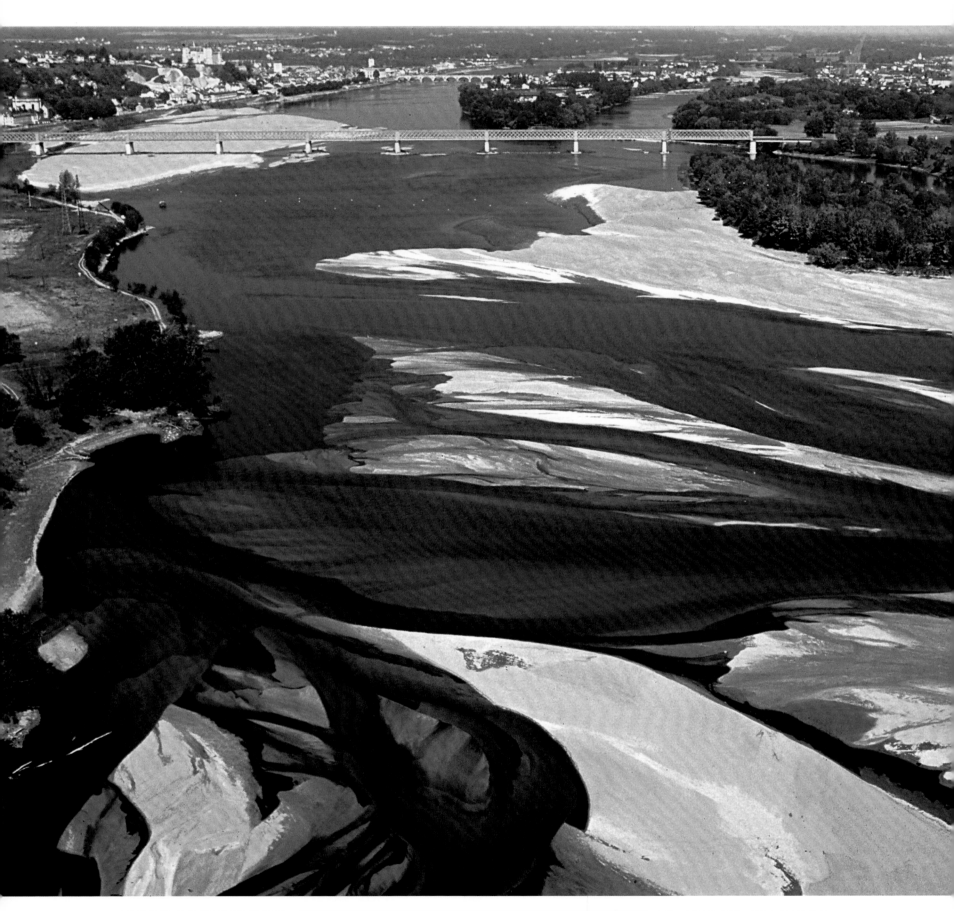

72-73 Large, shifting sandbars characterize the course of the Loire at Saumur, in the Maine-et-Loire department. The rather long distance between the opposite banks of the river has always discouraged the construction of bridges here, and in fact ferryboats were used at this point up to the mid-20th century.

72 bottom A canal flows lazily in the broad and humid plain that surrounds the basin formed by the Loire River estuary, which in the distant past was many times submerged by the sea. In fact, the tides go up the river for about 30 miles (50 km) into the interior, as far as the port of Nantes, the terminus of river navigation.

THE LOIRE

73 Before the construction of the impressive bridge at Mindin, transfer between St.-Nazaire and St.-Brévin was possible only via regular ferry service. The bridge, almost 2.2 miles (3.5 km) long, passes over the estuary of the Loire, while the towering central piers are no less than 425 ft (130 m) high. This impressive achievement of avant-garde engineeering has contributed to the commercial and urban development of the port of St.-Nazaire and the outlying zones, which constitute one of France's leading industrial hubs.

THE DANUBE

GATEWAY TO THE EAST

According to Greek mythology, the Argonauts, on their way back from their journey in search of the Golden Fleece, went up the Danube as far as the point closest to the Adriatic Sea, where they abandoned the river and carried their ships as far as the sea.

This legend highlights the main feature of the Danube, the only large European river that flows from West to East and empties into an inland sea. Since remote times this special characteristic has played a role in history making. The Danube is the gateway to the Orient; during the different historic epochs its valley has been the theater of contact, and often of conflict, between different cultures and peoples. However, unlike the Rhine, this huge natural corridor, constantly traveled by invading armies, has never been a true frontier, as have many of its tributaries, which have served as transverse barriers blocking penetration into the interior.

Coming from the remote steppes of Asia, the Avars and Huns ravaged Central Europe. Then came the Mongols, the fearsome warriors of the Anti-Christ: in 1241 they conquered the Hungarian city of Pest and on Christmas Day Batu Khan led his hordes over the frozen Danube and captured Esztergom, adrancing as far as the gates of Vienna. The Danube was also used by the Franks under Charlemagne and the Crusader armies heading to Jerusalem. The river was the strategic route taken by the Ottoman Turks during their *jihad* or holy war, when they almost overran the Christian West several times. Again, the Hapsburgs, Napoleon, Hitler's troops and the Red Army all fought along the Danube River. Lastly, the land bloodied by centuries of battles was enclosed by the Iron Curtain during the so-called Cold War. The Blue Danube of Viennese waltzes became red, politically speaking, split into two parts that were defended by barbed wire fences. Of all the world powers that fought for control of the river, only the ancient Romans managed to dominate it for any length of time from its sources to its mouth.

The second distinctive feature of the Danube is precisely its ungovernable nature: all attempts at making it an international river open to navigation and commerce for all nations have been in vain, coming up against harsh reality. Up to the fall of the Soviet regime and the division of Yugoslavia, eight nations and two opposing ideologies divided the waters of the Danube. From the Congress of Vienna in the early 1800s to the Conference of Belgrade in 1948, the treaties regulating the circulation of men and goods on the river were failures. Indeed, a dramatic aura seems to have enveloped the entire history of the Danube, up to the present. The ethnic conflicts and 'cleansing' in Yugoslavia, as well as the bombing of Belgrade on the part of the NATO forces, have awakened specters that we thought were definitively removed from the conscience of Europeans.

Moreover, the Danube has other problems of a purely practical nature. First of all, it is too long. In its 1798 miles (2900 km) from the Black Forest to the Dobrudja region in Romania, it crosses several different environments, so that its supply of water is irregular and its regimen extremely variable: low water stages and floods follow one another in quick, even sudden, succession, with changes in the river level that are sometimes drastic.

Then, to complicate matters there is the ice, which in the bitterly cold winter can block the flow of the river for weeks on end. In short, the Danube has a capricious nature, and it comes as no surprise that the volume of river traffic is barely 70 million tons per year, far below the 200 million of the Rhine. Needless to say, this comparison is unfair: the Rhine crosses the economic hubs of Europe and empties in the Rotterdam harbor, while the Danube ends its course in an inland body of water and passes through poorer countries that are worn out from too many years of being excluded from the global market. And yet the destinies of the two rivers are connected more than might seem at first sight. They are linked

74-75 *The medieval villages of Nagymaros and Visegrád, in Hungary, lie respectively on the left and right banks of the so-called Danube Bend. These villages contain important artistic and historic testimony of Hungary's past.*

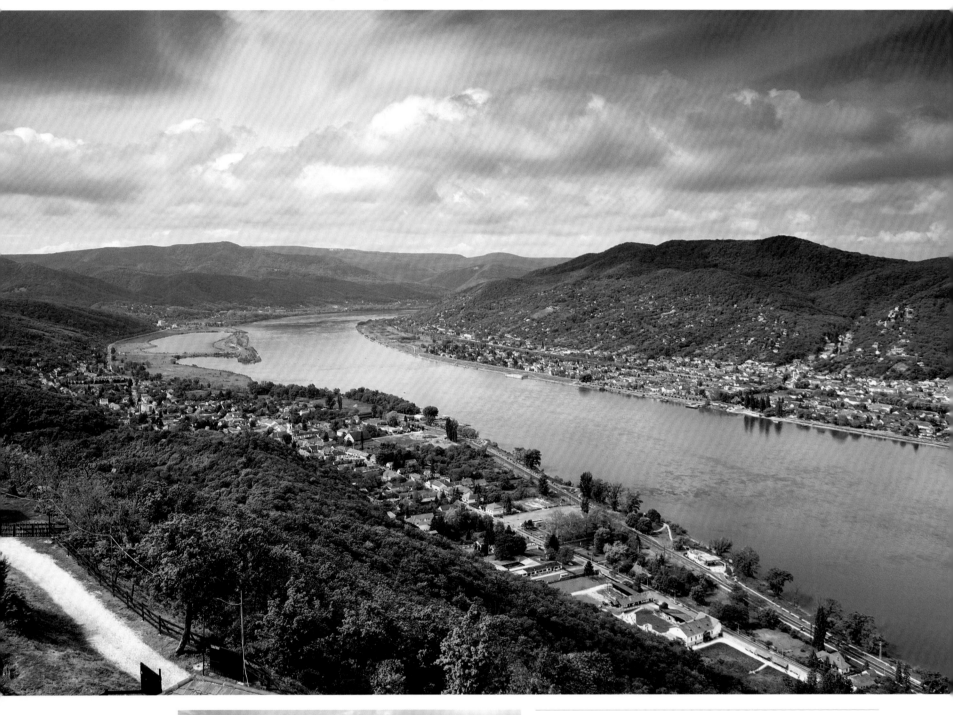

75 *bottom left After wandering for a long stretch among the green hills of Bavaria the Danube arrives at Kelheim, flowing into a narrow gorge that cuts through tall white limestone cliffs. Near the town the river merges with the large manmade canal that connects it with the River Main.*

75 *bottom right The Danube-Main canal with its intense barge traffic flows past the charming scenery of Bavaria. The idea of a waterway that would merge the two rivers was conceived as long ago as the age of Charlemagne, but work on the project was initiated only after the Second World War and was fraught with difficulties.*

not only by a very important canal, but above all by the plan of the new European Union, which is destined to include the Danubian nations in the future.

The Danube rises in the Black Forest, a short distance from the lower section of the Rhine, of which it is to a certain degree an affluent. The river is the result of the merger of two small torrents, the Brege and the Brigach, at Donaueschingen. At least, this is the official version, since the Danube, like all the other large rivers in the world, has a source linked with

becomes wider and meanders toward Kelheim, where there is an artificial canal that links it to the Main and then to the Rhine. The dream of a continental waterway that would connect the North Sea and the Black Sea is quite old: twelve centuries ago, at the behest of Charlemagne, thousands of laborers began to dig the so-called Carolingian Ditch, whose traces can still be seen around Nuremberg. Since that time the project was proposed several times, only to be abandoned once again. The work was finally finished and ceremoniously

tradition: popular legend ignored geography and identified the source as a Baroque fountain in the middle of a municipal park at Donaueschingen. A shapely goddess takes loving care of the river during its rather hesitant first steps. Soon afterward the river disappears underground, emerging again a few miles farther on. During its subterranean journey a part of its waters end up in the Rhine by means of mysterious passageways. When this short-lived secret love has ended, the Danube winds through the cultivated fields and wooded hills of southern Germany, and comes to its first encounter with a city, Ulm, the birthplace of Albert Einstein. The bell tower of the Gothic cathedral of Ulm is the tallest in the world, soaring in an ethereal ascent for 528 ft (160 m).

When it flows into the Regensburg plain, the Danube

inaugurated only in 1992, making it possible to navigate for all the 2170 miles (3500 km) that separate Rotterdam from the Danube drainage basin. Before the canal was opened, Regensburg, at the Danube's confluence with the Regen, was the last river port for large vessels. The beautiful Romanesque and Gothic churches, the town hall, and the luxurious patrician residences all bear witness to the former splendor of the city, which was a prosperous commercial center from the 10th century on.

At that time and up to the mid-1800s, navigating down the Danube was no simple matter. Shoals, strong currents and underwater obstacles often endangered the cargo and the very life of the merchants. The valley is often swept by westerly winds, which made it impossible to navigate on sailboats; the

77 bottom right The Danube reflects the profile of the impressive Renaissance castle in Neuburg, one of the most lively cultural towns in Bavaria.

76-77 Time seems to have stood still in the charming town of Ulm, in southern Germany.

77 bottom left The Benedictine abbey of Weltenburg, at Kelheim, is the oldest in Bavaria.

THE DANUBE

only way to go up the river was to tow the craft from the land with the aid of teams of oxen or horses. Bandits, predators and the heavy duty levied by many avid local lords were all an integral part of the risk involved in any journey down the Danube.

At Dassau the Danube receives a large amount of water from the Inn River and leaves Germany, entering Austrian territory. Once past the aristocratic city of Linz, it heads toward the Wachau Valley in what may be the most beautiful section of its long course. The river then runs slowly among the last slopes of the Alps, whose rocky skeleton sometimes

78 bottom The Inn, Ilz and
Danube rivers converge in the
Bavarian city of Passau, thus
splitting it into four distinct
zones that are linked by a series
of bridges. Passau Cathedral,
built in the 15th century and
drastically altered in the
Baroque period, is famous for
its colossal organ.

78-79 The castle in which Richard
Lion-Heart was kept prisoner keeps
watch over the town of Dürnstein,
on the left bank of the Danube.

79 bottom The town of Krems
lies along the Danube in the
Wachau Valley. In the
background is the Benedictine
abbey of Göttweig.

THE DANUBE

emerges suddenly from the thick woods. On the natural spurs that plunge headlong to the shores of the Danube there are medieval fortresses and monasteries: the Benedictine monastery at Melk, the castles of Schallaburg and Schönbuhel, and the ruins of the Dürnstein citadel.

The charming meadowland of Tulln introduces the Danube to Vienna, the last bulwark of the West centuries ago. In 1529 and 1683, the walls of this city managed to check the impetus of the Turkish armies. Vienna, the capital of the Hapsburg dynasty, boasts a wealth of splendid monuments and is the international temple of music: Gluck, Haydn, Mozart, Beethoven, Schubert, Brahms and Mahler brought fame to the city with their immortal compositions. The most famous of the 149 waltzes composed by Johann Strauss, *The Blue Danube*, has become the everlasting symbol of the carefree and gay Viennese lifestyle.

After Vienna, at the confluence with the Morava River, the last section of the eastern Carpathian Mts. forces the

80 top *The scenery along the course of the Danube in Wachau Valley is particularly enchanting in spring, when the apricot trees are blossoming. Famed for its excellent wines, this valley is one of the most popular tourist attractions in Austria.*

80 center *The Danube is a full-fledged river 985 ft (300 m) wide when it crosses the northern quarters of Vienna. The capital of Austria, one of the most important cities in Europe, extends in concentric circles around the famous Ring and St. Stephen's Cathedral.*

80 bottom *Situated on the banks of the Danube in the outskirts of Vienna, the modern buildings of the UNO-City contain the offices of prestigious organizations such as the International Atomic Energy Agency, OPEC (Organization of Petroleum Exporting Countries), and the United Nations Industrial Development Organization.*

80-81 *Intense commercial traffic does not disturb the silence of the virgin forests and marshes that flank the banks of the Danube near Vienna. Because of its marvelous natural scenery, this area, one of the last uncontaminated ones in Central Europe, has been declared a national park.*

81 bottom The unique shape of the castle of Bratislava rises up over the city, which is a major river port and the only commercial outlet of Slovakia on the Danube. At Bratislava, also known as Pressburg, Napoleon and Francis II of Austria signed a peace treaty in 1805.

82 top Belgrade, the capital of
Serbia, stands at the junction of the
Sava and the Danube. Given its
strategic position, this city has
suffered innumerable invasions and
much destruction.

82 center Buda, one of the two
cities that constitute Budapest,
lies on the low hills that border
the right bank of the Danube.
In the foreground is St. Matthias
Church.

E U R O P E

Danube into a narrow passage, the entrance to the vast
Hungarian lowlands, which extends for hundreds of miles
up to northern Serbia and the Romanian border. From
Bratislava to Esztergom the river forms the border between
Hungary and Slovakia. Then, making a sharp bend, it heads
southward into the fertile plains of Hungary. This is the
puszta, flat and uniform, without trees, once the breadbasket
of the Hapsburg Empire. Buda, on the right bank, and Pest
on the left one welcome the Danube with their royal
setting. Budapest, which was destroyed and rebuilt several
times, shows off its most beautiful monuments along the
riverside: the Fishermen's Bastion, the Neo-Gothic dome
and spires of the Parliament, the St. Matthias Church, and
the Buda Royal Palace, the residence of the Hungarian rulers
and the Hapsburgs. The Danube leaves Hungary at
Mohács, marking the Serbian-Croatian border. It was in the
nondescript plains of Mohács, in 1526, that Suleyman the
Magnificent routed the Hungarian army and established
Turkish dominion over the region for the following 160
years. When it reaches Belgrade, the Danube is at the
halfway point of its voyage to the sea, which it reaches with
a gradient of only 330 ft (100 m). In Serbia, three large
affluents, the Drava, Timis and Sava, increase the discharge
of the Danube considerably as it flows majestically toward
the mountains that can be seen in the distance. The Balkan
range and the massive arc of the Transylvanian Alps meet at
the Serbian-Romanian border, squeezing the Danube like
stone pincers: the gloomy ruins of Golubac castle herald the
deepest gorges in Europe, the Iron Gate, which is a little
more than 330 ft (100 m) wide. Up to a few decades ago
the river rushed furiously into this opening, swirling

THE DANUBE

82 bottom and 83 bottom A series of
bridges connects Buda and Pest, which
together form Budapest. Buda, on the
right bank of the river, began as a
fortified citadel after the Tatar invasion
of 1241; Pest, which was inhabited
by German-speaking immigrants, was
on the other hand a trade center for a
long period. The administrative union
of the two cities took place in 1873,
during Hapsburg rule.

82-83 The Hungarian
Parliament Building in
Budapest, with its rich Neo-
Gothic style, is one of the largest
in the world. It was built in
1904 during the reign of
Emperor Francis Joseph I of
Austria and Hungary. A short
way downstream the Danube
divides, with Margaret Island in
the center.

between the steep rock faces blanketed by thick forests. Eddies, currents and outcropping rocks and cliffs were a formidable obstacle to navigation. Since 1972 a large dam has checked the rush of the Danube, which flows into a placid artificial lake. Below it is welcomed by the vast Wallachian plain with its endless wheat and corn fields. The ancient Romans occupied this region in the 1st century AD, subjecting the local populations, which underwent thorough and long-lasting Romanization. For example, the Romanian language is Neo-Latin. The remains of the largest bridge in the Roman empire, built over the Danube by Emperor Trajan, 3960 ft (1200 m) and supported by twenty stone and cement piers, can still be seen near Turnu-Severin.

Once out of the Iron Gate, the river flows slowly in a valley that gradually becomes wider and more marshy: from Vidin to Silistra the Danube is once again a border, this time between Romania and Bulgaria. The Black Sea is quite near now, only 62 miles (100 km) away. But instead of forging straight ahead, the river turns northward, forming two branches. When it comes to Galati, it again changes direction and finally heads eastward, taking with it the waters of the Siret and the Prut, the last of the Danube's more than 300 affluents. The true river delta begins at Tulcea, where the Danube splits into three main branches: the Sulina, St. George and Kilya, which marks the border with the Ukraine. The endless expanse of rushes, the lakes, and the marshes that are the distinctive features of delta are an ideal habitat for an amazing variety of species of fish and migrating birds, which nest and mate there. This enormous natural oasis, which is virtually intact, is the farewell gift of the river to Europe. Beyond the last muddy beaches and the arc of islets bordering the river mouth, water and sky merge in a vague, indefinite horizon, where the Danube seems to dissolve into nothingness.

84 top right and 84-85 Over 250 species of birds find refuge in the marshland and swamps created by the Danube delta, which is the passageway of at least five major migratory routes and a crucial nesting and reproduction zone. Besides the northern and

Mediterranean species, there are cormorants, flamingoes, cranes and large groups of pelicans, which arrive from Asia and Africa. A true paradise of biodiversity, the Danube delta is a complex ecosystem many of whose secrets have not yet been revealed.

84 top left The meandering ravines known as the Iron Gate, which wind like a snake through the Carpathian Mts. and the Balkan hills, separate the course of the Danube in Serbia from its course in Romania. Here the river is often made choppy by the boat traffic.

85 bottom Fishing is one of the main activities of those who live in the Danube delta, which provides about half the freshwater fish sold in Romania. Over 100 species of fish populate the waters of the river and the large brackish lakes that dot the delta. Pollution and exploitation of the environment have brought about a decrease in the population of sturgeons, whose eggs are served as caviar. The Danube Delta Biosphere Reserve was recently established to try to make up for the harm done in the past.

84 center and bottom Sandy islets, stretches of aquatic plants and thick forests characterize the landscape of the Danube delta, one of the few places in Europe that are still locked in mystery. When it empties into the Black Sea in Romania, the river splits into three main branches that give rise to an intricate maze of small lakes and secondary canals that cover a surface area of about 1930 sq. miles (5000 sq. km). Because of the silt deposited by the river, the delta moves toward the sea at a rate of 130 ft (40 m) per year.

THE DUERO

THE FRONTIER OF FAITH

A few broken columns and the ruins of a patrician villa are all that remains of ancient Numantia, a few miles from Soria. Once the Romans had quenched the major rebellion of the Lusitani and Iberian Celts in the mid-2nd century BC, Rome became the undisputed ruler of the Iberian Peninsula. Only Numantia resisted, protected by its impregnable fortifications. In 134 BC, command of the military operations in northern Spain was entrusted to Scipio the Younger, the man who had razed Carthage to the ground, who decided there and then to capture the city by making it starve. He had all the surrounding countryside burned and the Duero River blocked by sharpened tree trunks, thus depriving the defenders of the city of their last supply line. Numantia fell after a nine-month siege. It was burned and utterly destroyed: rather than becoming prisoners of the Romans, most of the inhabitants committed suicide.

Soria is one of the provinces of Old Castile, a harsh land forged by the sun and the frost of the meseta, the rugged plateau in the heart of Spain. The churches and fortresses of Old Castile and León, whose boundary is the Duero, were the centers of the Christian struggle against the Moors, as the poets and heroes of the epic *reconquista* came from these two regions. In the poems celebrating El Cid Campeador, the Castilian tongue became literature and the national language. The character and culture of the Spanish were shaped in this dynamic mixture of history and legend, faith and pragmatism.

The Duero River rises on the wooded slopes of the Picos de Urbión, at the northern tip of the Iberian Mts., which separate its basin from that of the Ebro River. Flowing in a narrow and rocky valley, it arrives at the village of Duruelo de la Sierra, receiving the waters of numerous small torrents in its

descent. After Covaleda, the current becomes less rapid and the Duero flows in a broader bed, meandering toward Soria, which was once the eastern outpost of the Kingdom of Castile. The river, which in the Middle Ages marked the boundary with the regions under Muslim dominion, gradually becomes a fortified line: from Berlanga del Duero to Peñafiel, a series of monumental castles dominates the barren countryside of the plateau. Built on isolated rock spurs in the plain and surrounded by tall walls that end in a large quadrangular keep, all these fortresses were intended to be impregnable. One of them, situated at Gormaz, was where the military leader Rodrigo Diaz de Vivar, known as the Cid, began his violent career. When he was only twelve he killed the local lord to revenge himself and then married his young daughter. His life was a continuous series of duels, victorious battles against the Arabs, pilgrimages and meetings with saints, popes and kings. At least this is the story handed down by tradition. For historians, on the other hand, the Cid was nothing more than an adventurer, a soldier of fortune ready to offer his services to the best bidder, be he a Christian or Muslim.

The other aspect of Castile, mysticism and faith, appears in all its beauty in the constellation of monasteries, churches and abbeys that sanctify the Duero River Valley. The Romanesque façade of Santo Domingo Church at Soria is decorated with hundreds of statuettes that depict the main episodes in the Old and New Testament: standing out among the Apocalypse, the Passion of Christ, and the Massacre of the Innocents is the figure of Alfonso VII, the conqueror of Almería in 1147.

At Almazán the Duero suddenly changes direction, heading to the west. Here the network of canals allows the local population to irrigate hundreds of thousands of acres of

86 top In the stretch that marks the Spanish-Portuguese border, the Duero River penetrates a narrow canyon and flows between inaccessible rock faces that are hundreds of feet high. These are the Arribes del Duero, the most spectacular gorges formed by this river in its long course from the Sierra de Urbión to the Atlantic Ocean.

86-87 Cultivated fields and vineyards flank the Duero River near the peaceful town of Toro, in the Spanish province of Zamora. This land, which was once the theater of bloody battles between Christians and Muslims, produces some of the best wines in Spain.

87 bottom The vast, fertile plains of Castile-Léon near Gormaz are covered with wheat. The artificial lakes that interrupt the course of the Duero ensure large supplies of water for irrigation in a region that suffers from a chronic lack of rainfall.

88-89 Zamora, the capital of one of the nine regions that make up the province of Castile-León, lies on the banks of the Duero near the Spanish-Portuguese border. Among the noteworthy monuments in this city are the 12th-century cathedral and the 12th-century stone bridge over the Duero, which has sixteen graceful arches.

88 bottom A medieval bridge crosses the Duero at Tordesillas, in the province of Valladolid. The historic treaty whereby Spain and Portugal divided the newly discovered lands in the New World was signed in this city, which in that period was the seat of the Spanish court.

89 top Gormaz, lying on the banks of the Duero in the province of Soria, in one of the most picturesque parts of the borderland that witnessed the legendary exploits of El Cid Campeador. The hero of the Reconquista was rewarded by King Alfonso VI, who gave him the grandiose castle with 28 towers that dominates the village.

89 bottom Like a ship grounded on the plateaus that surround the Duero Valley, the castle of Peñafiel stands out at the eastern margins of Valladolid Province. The fortress, rebuilt in the early 14th century, is 656 ft (200 m) long and stands on the top of a rocky crest.

land that are used to grow cereals and as vineyards. The autonomous region of Castile-León is the largest wheat producer in Spain and the wines made in the Duero Valley are world-famous. The many dams that interrupt the course of the river provide a good supply of hydroelectric power and also act as reservoirs during droughts. The other areas of northern Spain often suffer from a scarcity of rainfall, and during the torrid continental summer most of the river evaporates. Furthermore, the river has an unstable and rather capricious regimen: in the past its outflow in the low- and high-water periods might vary from two to 700,000 cubic ft (20,000 cubic m) per second. Now, with the construction of a series of artificial basins, things have changed and the farmers of the meseta are better off. Yet the so-called Castile Canal was not laid out for irrigation, but for trade: by means of the Pisuerga River, an affluent of the Duero, the breadbasket of Spain sought an outlet toward Santander and the ports on the Bay of Biscay. Construction began in the late 1700s, during the reign of Ferdinand VI, and was completed only about 250 years later. Today the canal has revitalized the Tierra de Campos, with is 123,500 acres (50,000 hectares) of grain cultivation, and provides Valladolid with water. This city, the only large industrial center in the region, was once the capital of the empire and the favorite residence of the kings of Spain. Far from the opulence of court life, in a nondescript alley of Valladolid, Christopher Columbus died in 1506. And Miguel de Cervantes, plagued by misfortune and poverty, spent a brief period here in peace at work on his *Don Quixote*.

The Pisuerga, Valderaduey and above all the Esla, all flowing from the Cantabrian Mts., furnish a lot of water to the Duero, which continues its journey sluggishly through the undulating plains of the Castile basin. Tordesillas, on the right bank of the river, is a sleepy village with a few thousand inhabitants. And it was the venue, in 1494, of the signing of the treaty that for the first time divided the world

into two spheres of influence: through the offices of the pope, the *raya*, an imaginary meridian line that divided the Atlantic Ocean, was marked out. Spain had the right to own all the lands discovered west of that virtual boundary, while Portugal had a free hand to the east of the line.

Once past Zamora, the river changes its look. Its gradient increases and the current becomes swifter. The Arribas del Duero, 78 miles (120 km) of dizzying gorges squeezed between precipitous rock faces hundreds of feet high, mark the most spectacular section of the Spanish-Portuguese border.

Eagles, vultures, black storks, and peregrine falcons populate the valley, and the craggy cliffs of the surrounding mountains are the home of the last packs of wolves in the Iberian Peninsula.

When the river flows into Portugal it takes the name of Duoro. Terraces with vineyards cover the steep, sunny shores. Port wine, the pride and joy of the national winemaking tradition, is produced in this area. Fortified with the addition of brandy, which interrupts the process of fermentation and preserves the sugar content, the port is poured into wooden barrels and aged until it has the right quality. After 573 miles (925 km), the Duoro flows into the Atlantic Ocean at Oporto, the mother city of Portugal.

90-91 and 91 bottom left After having formed part of the Spanish-Portuguese border, the Duero flows into Portugal, where it is called the Douro. The hills that roll down toward the river are covered with vineyards: the world-famous port wine is produced in this thin strip of land between the towns of Mazouco and Barqueiro that is no more than 18 miles (30 km) wide.

91 bottom right With their veils unfurled and decorated with the brand-names of the main producers of port, these barcos rabelos proceed slowly in the Douro river in the city of Oporto, Portugal. Up to 1965 these traditional flat-bottomed sailboats were used to transport wine on the river.

THE DUERO

THE PO

FROM THE ALPS TO THE SEA

Compared to the other European rivers, the Po seems almost insignificant. It is not a major commercial thoroughfare like the Rhine, nor has it the historic importance of the Danube or the Seine. And compared to the powerful Volga it looks like a mere brook. Its importance does not depend on its size or discharge, but on the land it traverses. The Po River Valley is the center of gravity of the Italian economy and one of the richest and most densely populated areas in Europe: one-third of the agricultural, zootechnical and industrial production of Italy is concentrated in the Po basin, where some 16 million people live and work. The river provides this huge population with electric power and water to irrigate the farmland and rice paddies; at the same time it is a major vacation and recreation area. From the French border to the lowlands of the Po Delta, a chain of cities dots the shores of this great river: industrial centers such as Turin, the home of the FIAT automobile-manufacturers, and lovely art cities such as Piacenza, Pavia, Cremona, Mantua and Ferrara.

Padania, the valley of the Po (which the Romans called the Padus), is in every respect a gift from the river. A million years ago the plain lay under a warm, shallow sea that ran as far as the edges of the pre-alpine mountains in the region of Piedmont. Then the Earth's crust slowly rose and the climate became rainier. The erosive action of the rivers increased, gradually filling the enormous basin with sediment so that it became flat and uniform. The Po divides the Po River Valley into two asymmetrical sections. In fact, the combined force of the Alpine affluents, which are much swifter and larger than the Apennine tributaries, has shifted it course southward. This two-fold supply determines the regular regimen of the river, which in spring is replenished by the thawing snow on the Alps and in autumn by the floodwater that swells the waterways from the Apennines. However, the placid aspect of the Po must not delude us, because despite the fact that the river, from Cremona onward, flows between tall embankments, its floods have often had devastating effects. In November 1951 the river broke through the embankments below Ferrara, inundating most of the Polesine area with 10 ft (3 m) of muddy water; the result was a single

lake ranging from Rovigo to Adria and as far as the Adige River. The last flood struck the Piedmont region in 2000: after three days of terrific rainfall, the floodwaters overran vast zones of Turin. The water supply had to be suspended, the bridges were closed, and road and railway transportation was interrupted. The Dora Baltea, Orco and other minor tributaries overflowed over the countryside. The toll reads ten deaths, 10,000 people homeless, and 500,000 euros of damage to the infrastructures.

The cause of this disaster begins almost secretly, as it were, with typical Piedmontese modesty, from the slopes of a perfect mountain, Monviso, which towers over the Cottian Alps. At Pian del Re, between two rock masses covered with lichens, a commemorative plaque officially indicates the origin of the Po, even specifying the altitude – 6666 ft (2020 m) above sea level. But the true source of the river is even higher, consisting of a series of torrents and small lakes with their distributaries that merge above the village of Crissolo. The river plunges headlong downstream, with a gradient of 4950 ft in only 22 miles (1500 m in only 35 km). Revello and Saluzzo welcome it at the threshold of the pre-Alpine plain. In the late 15th century the old salt road passed through the valley, completing its journey from the Rhône River delta to the marches of the marquisate of Saluzzo. The monumental Staffarda Abbey marks the beginning of the middle section of the Po, which from here heads directly northward. The river widens in a vast and winding bed, flowing through an expanse of farmland with intensive cultivation. The profile of the Alps fades away in the distance and the first rows of poplars appear on the scene. Before arriving at Turin, the Po receives three Alpine affluents – the Maira, Varaita and Pellice – which increase its outflow to a considerable degree.

The relationship between the Po and Turin is rather recent; the city began to expand beyond the historic center only during the Napoleonic period. The major city thoroughfare, Via Po, and the Neo-Classical Piazza Vittorio, which directly faces the river, both date from the early 1800s. Once past Turin, the Po flows eastward, touching the beautiful hills of the Monferrato and Oltrepò Pavese areas. At Chivasso, the Cavour Canal connects the Po with the Ticino River, channeling part of its

92 top The monumental Umberto I Bridge, built in the early 20th century, crosses over the Po River in Turin, connecting the downtown area and the Porta Nuova railway station with the hilly areas. It is decorated with four statues representing Compassion, Valor, Art and Labor.

92-93 Viewed from the Superga Basilica situated on the hill that borders the right bank of the Po, the plain on which Turin develops fades away toward the foothills of the Alps. The Po crosses the city from south to north, taking in the waters of the Sangone, Dora Riparia and Stura di Lanzo rivers.

93 bottom The fascinating profile of the Borgo Medievale, immersed in the greenery of the Valentino Park, welcomes the Po on its entrance into Turin. This impressive edifice was built on occasion of the International Exposition of 1884 as a reproduction of a slice of 15th-century life in the Piedmont region.

THE PO

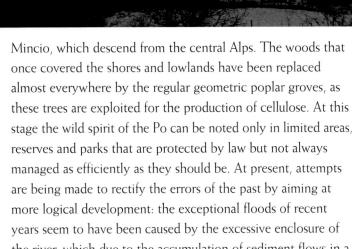

water to the rice fields in the Vercelli region. After the confluence with the Sesia and Tanaro rivers, the Po runs into the great plain. Then the merger with the Ticino makes it majestic and solemn: the pebbly banks give way to the large and ever-changing sandy ones. Massive embankments, which are often quite a distance from the shores, accompany the river, which now flows in a single channel.

From the 10th century on, the Benedictine and Cistercian monks began to reclaim the marshland situated along the Po. But only in the early 1900s was this humid zone successfully transformed into land fit for agriculture, a process that reshaped the lower Po Valley landscape. Above Piacenza the last strip of the Ligurian Apennines stretches out toward the river, separating the Marengo plain from the Emilia region. In that narrow passage near the confluence with the Trebbia River, Hannibal enjoyed his first major victory over the Romans in 218 BC. In the area between Piacenza and Mantua, the Po receives three of the largest of its 141 tributaries: the Adda, the Oglio and the

Mincio, which descend from the central Alps. The woods that once covered the shores and lowlands have been replaced almost everywhere by the regular geometric poplar groves, as these trees are exploited for the production of cellulose. At this stage the wild spirit of the Po can be noted only in limited areas, reserves and parks that are protected by law but not always managed as efficiently as they should be. At present, attempts are being made to rectify the errors of the past by aiming at more logical development: the exceptional floods of recent years seem to have been caused by the excessive enclosure of the river, which due to the accumulation of sediment flows in a bed that is higher than the surrounding plains. The delta, on the contrary, is slowly sinking below sea level. The Po arrives at the Adriatic Sea with fourteen mouths and inlets fed by five large delta branches. The labyrinth of lagoons, canebrakes and forests has created one of the most interesting environments in Europe. For twenty years there has been talk of a Po Delta National Park. The river, melancholy, hopes that better times are ahead.

95 bottom left The middle course of the Po, from Turin to Ferrara, is vital for Po River Valley agriculture. Here we see corn and soy fields in the Mantua area.

95 bottom right The Po, fed abundantly by its tributaries, flows majestically among large sand bars in the Piedmont plain downstream from Turin.

94 top In winter the small vessels used for going down the Po at the Piedmont-Lombardy border remain moored on the banks.

94 bottom and 94-95 The rice paddies in the area between the Po, the Sesia and the Ticino rivers flood over in spring. In winter, after the harvest, the water is replaced by a layer of frost.

97 center bottom Only the occasional fisherman's home interrupts the monotony of the horizon in the Valli di Comacchio area, which consists of vast lagoons with still waters formed by the configuration of the Po delta.

97 bottom The Este castle of Mesola, in the province of Ferrara, was built in the late 1500s on the right bank of the Po di Goro, one of the main branches of the delta. Surrounded by a 7.5 mile (12-km) wall, this castle was used as both a summer residence and hunting lodge.

96-97 The Trebbia River merges with the Po upstream from Piacenza, the capital of the westernmost province of the Emilia-Romagna region.

96 bottom The bridges over the Po River are the weak point of the road and railway communications system of the Po Valley, the hub of the Italian economy.

97 top The 'skyline' of Cremona, which overlooks the Po, stands out against the hazy sky of the lower Po Valley.

97 center top Fishing has always been one of the main economic activies of the Po River delta. In the Valli di Comacchio the fishermen still use the traditional method of the lavorieri, *wedge-shaped barriers that capture the migrating eels and fish in the delta.*

great rivers
AFRICA
of the world

We need take only a quick glance at a map of Africa to realize that the network of rivers there reflects the climatic conditions and geographic configuration of the continent.

Africa south of the Sahara Desert is like a large tableland, which is bordered by steep cliffs, especially in the southern section. Consequently, near their mouths all the African rivers are interrupted by swift or spectacular waterfalls that impede navigation. The fact that the rivers cannot therefore be used to penetrate the interior, together with the difficulties and obstacles posed by the environment, made the exploration of the African continent a long and arduous undertaking. Up to about 150 years ago, the heart of the continent was like a huge white blotch on the maps. The sources of the Nile River, the greatest geographic puzzle of all time, were unknown for twenty centuries. And the Blue Nile Valley, lost among the craggy hills of Ethiopia, was traced only in 1968 by an expedition of English soldiers who were provided with a great deal of logistical means and support. Most of the waterways and lakes are concentrated near the Equator, where there is abundant rainfall all year long. With the exception of the Congo, all the rivers in Africa are subject to periods of a shortage of water, with remarkable differences in the outflow between the dry and

rainy seasons. The waterway system in the Sahara zone is chaotic, reduced to a network of dry beds that only on exceptional occasions are filled with water.

The Niger and Senegal are the only important rivers in this section of West Africa and part of their course is situated in wholly arid zones. In the deserts of southern Africa the same configuration is repeated symmetrically, albeit in a less drastic fashion: the Okavango River, which begins in the hills of Angola, ends in the sands of the Kalahari Desert, creating a gigantic delta that in the years with heavy rainfall overflows into the dry basins in the middle of Botswana. Lake Etosha, on the other hand, has become dry for good, an absolutely sterile saline basin: its only tributary from the north was 'pirated' by the Cunene River, which flow into the Atlantic at the Angola-Namibia border. And according to the prediction of geologists, the Logoné River, which empties into Lake Chad, is about to end up the same way: its waters are feeding the Bénoué, and hence the Niger, to an ever increasing degree, and without it Lake Chad will become extinct. Except for the Zambesi, the only rivers of any importance in southern Africa are the Limpopo and the Orange, which descend from the Drakensberg Mts. and flows into the Atlantic Ocean some 1240 miles (2000 km) distant.

98 left *The Zambesi at Victoria Falls, in Zimbabwe.*

98 center *The mouth of the Congo River at Brazzaville, in the Congo.*

98 right *The temples of Abu Simbel on Lake Nasser, Egypt.*

99 *A fishermen's village on the banks of the Niger, in Nigeria.*

THE NILE

THE FATHER OF CIVILIZATION

The Nile is the longest river in the world, extending 4135 miles (6670 km), and certainly the most famous. No other geographic phenomenon has been wrapped in mystery for so long or has so fascinated people as the sources of this river. From a practical standpoint, the Nile is a complex hydraulic machine that carries the equatorial rainfall as far as the Mediterranean coast, after traversing the largest desert on Earth. Every year, at the end of the dry season, the river emerged from its bed and flooded the plains of ancient Egypt, depositing fertile silt that made for soil replenishment and thus brought prosperity in its wake. Indeed, the lives of millions of people depended on this miracle. And yet the ancient Egyptians never really bothered to find out where all that water came from, accepting it with a fatalistic attitude as a great gift from the gods. True, the level of the Nile was accurately measured by means of Nilometers in order to calculate the taxes to be levied on the landowners who benefited from the precious silt transported by the river, but this was all the ancients did.

The first people to be curious about the sources of the Nile were the ancient Greeks. Herodotus went up the river as far as Aswan, at which point he realized that going any farther was far beyond his capacities. The Romans fared no better with their expeditions. According to Ptolemy, the leading geographer of the time, the Nile rose at the so-called Mountains of the Moon, which were very high and covered with perennial snow. He drew up his famous map in the 2nd century AD, charting the course of the river with astonishing precision. Then, for the following 1700 years no significant datum was added to the knowledge of the river. The heart of Africa remained an imaginary place, the domain of monstrous creatures and cannibals. It was only on the threshold of the 19th century that an exploration mania pervaded Europe and the mystery of the source of the Nile suddenly became a topical subject.

In 1862 the members of the Royal Geographic Society of London were amazed to read a telegram sent from one of their emissaries in Africa. The message, signed by John Speke, was quite succinct: "The Nile has been sorted out." Naturally, the problem by no means solved. Speke had seen a large river flowing from Lake Victoria, but he had no proof that it was the Nile. For decades expeditions had set out in search of the source of the Nile despite incredible difficulties. Richard Burton, J. A. Grant, Samuel Baker, David Livingstone, Henry Stanley and other explorers of the time confronted this challenge, each one seeking his own personal source and a bit of glory. Spurred on by his detractors, Speke died in a hunting accident that had all the earmarks of suicide. A few years later, a plaque with a rather ambiguous inscription was set at the point where the Nile emerges from Lake Victoria: "Speke discovered this source of the Nile on 28 July 1862." Poor Speke had been partly right, as had Ptolemy, for that matter. And Baker, who found the source of the river in Lake Albert, was not far from the truth.

100 Rapids and falls are a distinguishing feature of the upper Kagera River, the most important tributary of Lake Victoria. The headstreams of the Kagera, now considered Nile's true source, rise on the mountains at an altitude of about 7900 ft (2000 m). They were discovered in 1937 by the German explorer Burkhart Waldecker.

100-101 After passing through Lake Victoria, the Nile enters forests of Uganda, the first stage in the long journey that ends in the Mediterranean Sea. The Ripon Falls, which the English explorer Speke asserted were the source of the Nile (1862), are now submerged by the waters of a large artificial lake.

101 bottom After the Owen Falls dam, the river, which is now about 985 ft (300 m) wide, flows through a narrow valley, creating a series of raging rapids among low hills covered with grass and patches of luxuriant vegetation.

THE NILE

102-103 and 103 center A thick forest covers the shores of Lake Victoria, by far the largest of the many natural basins that dot Equatorial Africa: a colossal inland sea 230 miles long by 155 miles wide (370 by 250 km) that adjoins the territories of Uganda, Kenya and Tanzania. A strong current runs through the lake from the mouth of the Kagera River to the exit of the Nile.

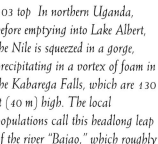

102 bottom and 103 bottom Large flocks of aquatic birds frequent the indented shores of Lake Victoria, which is bordered by luxuriant vegetation and marshland. The basin that hosts the waters of this enormous lake, which covers about 27,080 sq. miles

(70,000 sq. km), is the result of massive tectonic movements that led to the formation of the Great Rift Valley. The lake, named after the Britain's queen in the 19th century, is called Nyanza by the natives, which literally means 'water.'

103 top In northern Uganda, before emptying into Lake Albert, the Nile is squeezed in a gorge, precipitating in a vortex of foam in the Kabarega Falls, which are 130 ft (40 m) high. The local populations call this headlong leap of the river "Bajao," which roughly means 'the Devil's Cauldron.'

In fact, the situation is complex. Since 1937 the official source of the Nile has been established among the mountains of Burundi – the Kagera River, which is the most important inflowing waterway of Lake Victoria. A pyramid of stones symbolically sanctions its historic identity. Starting off from that inland sea, which is twice as large as Switzerland, the river begins it northward course, a direction it will maintain to a greater or lesser degree for its entire length. Crossing the hills of Uganda, the so-called Victoria Nile flows into the marshy Kyoga Lake and eventually reaches Lake Albert, the last of the chain of basins that dot the western Great Rift Valley.

The other branch of the genealogical tree of the Nile begins at Lake George, connected to Lake Edward, which in turn communicates with Lake Albert by means of the Semliki River. This section of the river system is fed by the rains that fall all year long on the Ruwenzori massif, the mythical Mountains of the Moon. Although it is rather distant from the remotest sources, Lake Albert is one of the two large reservoirs that collect the water that later gives rise to the Bahr el-Jebel, the Nile of the Mountains, which from this point on begins its voyage toward the lowlands of the Sudan. About 140 years ago, Baker guessed the truth, but strangely enough he limited his exploration to the northern tip of the lake, without bothering to prove his theory.

Baker is credited with the discovery of the Kabarega Falls, which brusquely interrupt the course of the Victoria Nile 31 miles (50 km) before the mouth in Lake Albert. All of a sudden, the river is squeezed between two walls of black rock and precipitates for 132 ft (40 m) into a ravine that is barely 20 ft (6 m) wide. A short distance downstream from the falls, where the current becomes placid, hundreds of crocodiles and hippopotami bask in the sun on beaches of golden sand. For years civil war raged in this region and was extremely harmful for the wild animals. The elephants and rhinoceroses, which abounded here even outside the confines of the national parks, were decimated by greedy hunters for

their ivory and horns, and poaching triggered by hunger did the rest. Recently the situation has improved greatly, and for Uganda, considered the "pearl of Africa" in the past, better times lie ahead.

Once past the Fula rapids, the Nile moves into the

THE NILE

Sudanese plains, a flat sea of grass dotted with acacias and thorny bushes that during the rainy season becomes a luxuriant savanna soaked with water. Juba is the capital of this solitary land that is periodically struck by rebellions against the excessive power wielded by Khartoum, which has always considered the Bilad-es-Sudan, or Land of the Blacks, a treasure trove of natural resources. Once it was the source of ivory and slaves, while now it provides minerals, petroleum and above all water, the most precious resource of all. A boat connects Juba and Kosti, 930 miles (1500 km) to the north, an exhausting journey that may take 8 to 10 days. No one knows how long it takes to navigate

through the swamps in the Bor Valley stretch of the Nile. The Arabs call them Sudd or 'obstacle,' while Baker gave them the name of the river of Hades, Styx: an aquatic maze as large as the Po River valley, a morass of water hyacinths, rushes and floating islands in continuous movement. For the explorers and traders who went up the river from Khartoum the Sudd swamps were a nightmare. In 1880 the Italian Romolo Gessi was trapped there for months; only one-fourth of the 600 men in his expedition managed to survive. The Nile risks disappearing in that maze of canals and lagoons that is really an inland delta, and when it emerges from the swamps its discharge has been reduced by half.

The Jonglei canal has been a topic of discussion for a century: it was supposed to divert the Nile for 230 miles (370 km), from Bor to the harbor of the Malakal River, taking its waters to the dry land of the northern Sudan and avoiding the swamps. Work on the canal began about twenty years ago, but it was interrupted by a series of targeted guerrilla attacks: the people in the south do not approve of the government project because they feel their land is being exploited without their gaining anything in return.

Isolated from the rest of the world, the Dinka, Nuer and Shilluk tribes live on livestock and fishing, while agriculture is practiced at a subsistence level. The economy of these populations, which are closely related, is based on animal husbandry. For them cows are everything – the heart of their social activities, the object of ardent love, and a yardstick for their relations with the world. The Dinka have 750 ways of describing the virtues of an animal, according to its size, color, the shape of its horns and ears, its character, and anything else that might satisfy the fertile imagination of pastoral people. The summer rainfall transforms

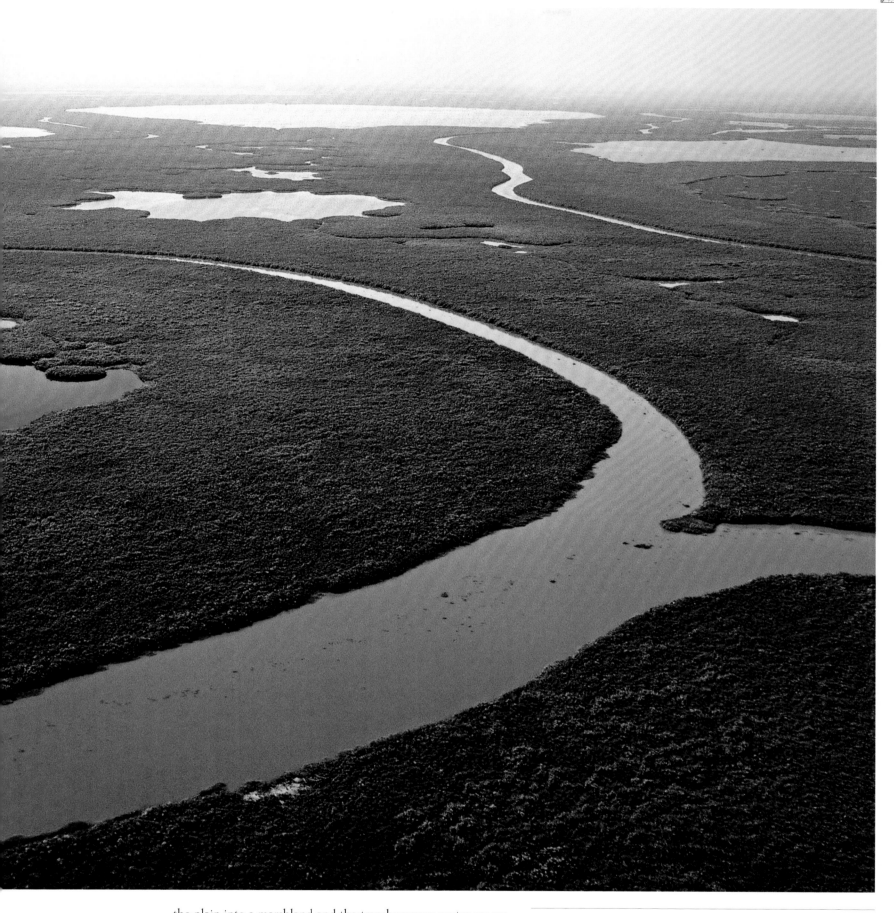

the plain into a marshland and the transhumance routes are no longer negotiable, so that the locals' life is concentrated in the villages, which are build in the elevated areas and surrounded by fields of millet and sorghum. Lake No, situated at the confluence with the Bahr el-Ghazal or Gazelle River, marks the end of the Sudd. A short distance farther on the Nile merges with the Giraffe River and also takes in the abundant waters of the Sobat, which arrives from the highlands of Ethiopia. From this point on, the river is known as the White Nile.

Passing Malakal, the river proceeds in a rather straight line

104 A felucca, the typical lateen-rigged sailing boat used for centuries on the lower course of the Nile, plows through the waters of the great river between Khartoum and Lake Nasser. Because of their shallow draft, feluccas are still the vessels most used for transporting goods in Sudan.

104-105 Viewed from on high, the Sudd swamps in southern Sudan look like a gigantic aquatic labyrinth with indefinite contours. Although they obstruct navigation along the Nile, the huge floating islands of papyrus and water hyacinths are the ideal habitat for a great many species of birds.

through countryside that gradually becomes more arid: the savannas are replaced by monotonous horizons that herald the desert. Christian and animistic Black Africa is about to give way to Islam. When it arrives at Khartoum, the capital of the Sudan, the White Nile flows slowly on a vast bed between muddy banks. The plant detritus it has collected while passing through the swamps imparts a milky color to the river. The Blue Nile, filled with dark silt, plunges turbulently into the White Nile and like a dam checks its current, which almost seems forced to retreat. From its source in the heart of the Ethiopian highlands,

it has flowed rapidly for about 992 miles (1600 km), taking in hundreds of streams and small tributaries along the way.

The Blue Nile begins at an altitude of 9500 ft (2900 m) in the Gojjam Mts.; the source, a spring with clear, freezing water, is considered sacred by the inhabitants of the highlands. At first the Blue Nile is nothing more than a stream that soon becomes muddy, but when it rises out of Lake Tana it is able to give a demonstration of its character. In a maelstrom of mist it precipitates for 165 ft (50 m) in the Tisisat Falls and then flows in a series of gorges, where it will remain for the rest of its long

106-107 The Blue Nile runs through the deeply eroded, almost lunar terrain of the Ethiopian highlands. For 500 miles (800 km) the river is inaccessible as it flows violently through a narrow canyon between tall basalt rock faces that may be as much as 3280 ft (1000m) high.

107 During the dry months the discharge of the Blue Nile is reduced to 350 cu. ft (10 cu. m) per second, and it flows placidly through the hills of Ethiopia (photograph above). The landscape of the valley floor changes drastically during the rainy season (photo below), when the river takes in forty times more water than before. The huge quantity of silt transported by the flow is what makes the Sudanese and Egyptian terrain near the river so amazingly fertile.

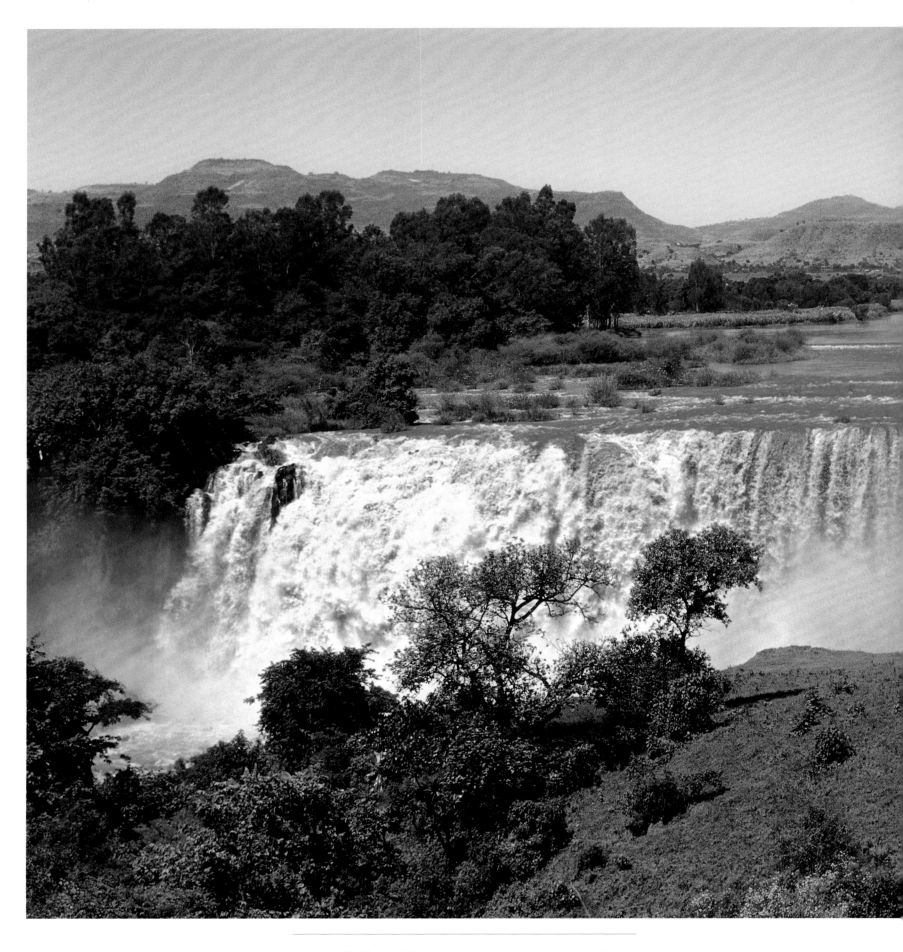

108-109 *The Tisisat Falls, among the most spectacular in Africa, interrupt the course of the Blue Nile barely 6.7 miles (10 km) downstream from Lake Tana. The river, which is 1640 ft (500 m) wide at this point, crashes against the rocks of its bed in a vortex of mist that is visible from a great distance.*

109 *From time immemorial the characteristic* tankwa, *very light boats made entirely of papyrus, have been used on the waters of Lake Tana, the natural reservoir of the Blue Nile. The lake covers a surface area of about 1390 sq. miles (3600 sq. km) and has a maximum depth of 45 ft (14 m).*

THE NILE

journey through Ethiopia. At certain points, the walls of the gorge created by the river are almost a mile (1.5 km) high. The valley floor is virtually inaccessible and the rapids make navigation dangerous. After the Sudan border, the Roseires Dam gathers the rushing water of the river in a vast artificial basin. The plantations of Gezira (the island) – hundreds of thousands of acres of land yielding cereals, peanuts, sugar cane and cotton

– are irrigated by the Blue Nile by means of a network of canals. This huge triangle of fertile land situated between the Blue and White Nile represents the Sudan's hope for a better future.

Despite the fact that part of its energy flows into the Gezira fields, the Blue Nile retains a considerable amount of water, which its 'elder brother' (the White Nile) needs in order to cross the Sahara Desert. The Atbara River, another Ethiopian tributary, also contributes a large amount of water. But even this would not be enough to guarantee the survival of the Nile if another element did not come into play at this point: in the Sahara stretch, the river follows a sort of natural canal or entrenched valley with walls of rock that prevent the water from flowing outwardly. Thanks to these factors, unlike all the other rivers that once crossed the Sahara Desert, the Nile has continued to flow even in the most arid periods.

The river banks between Khartoum and Akasha were the home of the kingdoms of Kush, which over 25 centuries ago dominated vast regions of Nubia and even Egypt: pyramids,

The Nile

110-111 *Villages, cultivated fields and palm groves flank the Nile between Aswan and Luxor. The river flows quietly through a broad, rather flat valley, past many marvelous temples that bear witness to the grandeur of ancient Egypt.*

110 bottom *Having reached Aswan after a journey of over 2485 miles (4000 km), the Nile flows proudly into Egypt. Its valley becomes a fertile strip of land no more than 12.5 miles (20 km) wide, surrounded by the Saharan sands and low rocky hills calcified by the sun.*

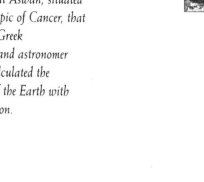

111 top The enormous basin of Lake Nasser, formed by the waters of the Nile upstream from the Aswan Dam, extends for over 310 miles (500 km) in the Nubian deserts. The lake contains about 6 billion cu. ft (170 million cu. m) of water, enough to cover the needs of Egypt in case of drought.

111 bottom An archipelago of rocky islets rises up from the blue waters of the Nile at Aswan, ancient Syene, at the threshold of Nubia. It was at Aswan, situated right on the Tropic of Cancer, that in 230 BC the Greek mathematician and astronomer Eratosthenes calculated the circumference of the Earth with amazing precision.

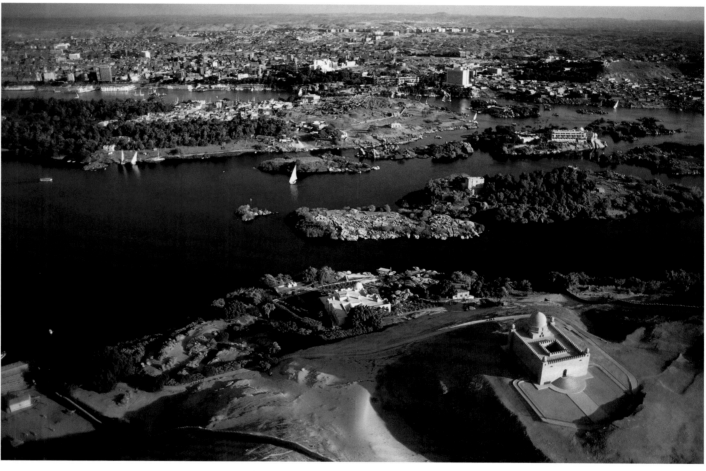

temples, and ruins of cities emerge from the desert at Meroe, Naga, Musawwarat, and Karima. In this region, which was once a major caravan crossroads, the Nile becomes a large, wide "S." Today much of Lower Nubia lies submerged by Lake Nasser, one of the largest artificial basins in Africa. Some 90,000 people were evacuated from the area and thanks to UNESCO, the temples of Abu Simbel were cut into blocks, removed and transported to a site 198 ft (60 m) higher up, in one of the most daring archaeological rescue operations ever carried out.

The Aswan Dam, built in the 1960s, has liberated Egypt from the caprices of the Nile, laying the foundation for rational agricultural and industrial development that was inconceivable in the past. The famine that periodically struck the Nile Valley is now a thing of the past. However, on the other side of the coin, the silt is trapped by the walls of the dam and no longer fertilizes the land, which is now threatened by the emergence of salt deposits. Deprived of the silt carried by the Nile floods, the delta is endangered by the erosion of the sea and is receding at an alarming rate. Many species of fish have disappeared and the stagnant water favors the spread of dangerous diseases. After the Aswan Dam the Nile flows placidly in a very soft countryside. The 744 miles (1200 km) that separate it from the sea are an extraordinary journey into the past. Edfu, Kom Ombo, Thebes, Karnak and the Valley of the Kings, where in 1922 the tomb of Tutankhamon was discovered: the monumental Egypt of the pharaohs passes slowly before you along the banks of the Nile. The ruins of temples, colossal statues, and columns are less concentrated as one gradually approaches Cairo. A short distance past the capital, the Nile branches off into two main arms, the Rosetta and Damietta, forming a triangle. The ancient Greek geographers called this a delta, like the fourth letter of their alphabet – a worthy epilogue for a grand river.

THE NILE

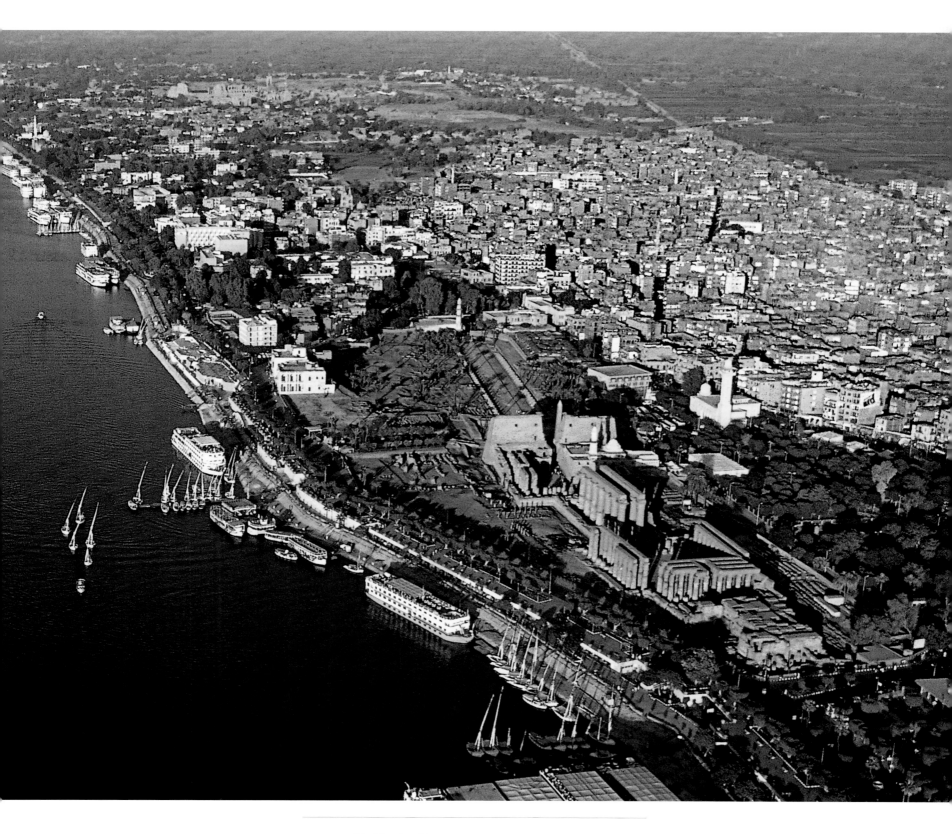

112-113 *The Temple of Luxor rises up majestically on the east bank of the Nile, which is crowded with boats of all kinds. Besides the temple, other easily recognizable monuments are the* *sanctuary of Amenhotep III, the great colonnade, the monumental pylons of Ramesses II and part of the avenue lined with sphinxes that connected the edifice with the Temple of Karnak.*

114-115 Cultivated fields surround one of the wide bends of the Nile in the vicinity of its delta in the Mediterranean.

115 top The feluccas with their white triangular sails are one of the distinguishing features of the Nile Delta landscape.

115 center top Large traffic-congested arteries and modern bridges over the Nile connect the residential areas of Zamalek, on the island of Roda, with 'downtown' Cairo.

115 center bottom Hundreds of islets covered with aquatic vegetation dot the surface of Lake Manzala, which extends from the Damietta branch of the Nile to Port Said, at the entrance of the Suez Canal. A thin strip of land separates the shallow brackish lagoon from the Mediterranean Sea.

115 bottom Viewed from above, the Nile Delta looks like a perfect fan, decorated with a 'necklace' of brackish lagoons, extending over 8880 sq. miles (23,000 sq. km). Seen here are the two main branches of the river, the Damietta and Rosetta Channels, at left and right respectively.

THE NILE

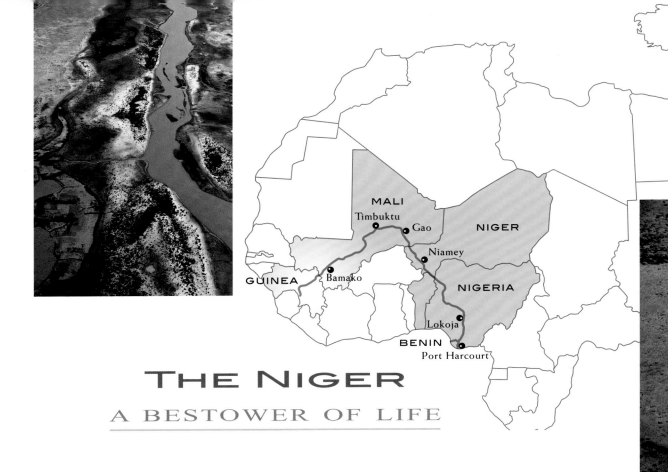

THE NIGER

A BESTOWER OF LIFE

After the Nile and Congo, the Niger is the third longest river in Africa, measuring 2585 miles (4170 km). Its course, interrupted below Ségou by an enormous inland delta, makes a broad bend through the heart of West Africa, from the mountains of Guinea to the Bight of Biafra.

The apex of this curve even penetrates the Sahara Desert, bringing water and life to one of the most barren and hottest regions on Earth. During its seemingly interminable journey the river crosses an extraordinary variety of environments: the rain forest, the Sudanese savanna, the Sahel region, and lastly the desert, then repeating the same pattern backwards.

In a period that roughly corresponds to our Middle Ages, the huge bend of the Niger, at the border between the nomadic and sedentary worlds, became the hub of flourishing trans-Saharan traffic: slaves, agricultural products from the savanna, and above all gold were transported along the caravan routes to the Mediterranean, while from the north there arrived salt, dates, copper and luxury goods. An urban civilization with new, characteristic features rose up and developed along the shores of the river: the empires of Mali and Songhai dominated vast territories and were part of the gigantic Islamic trade network that extended from Spain to distant Indonesia.

The Niger River was both the actual and symbolic hub around which the various components of this political and commercial complex congregated. In keeping with the anthropomorphic model of African tradition, Djenné and the other cities in the inland delta were considered the womb of an immense upside-down figure, the head of which was represented by Timbuktu, the rational mind that stood for the cultural and religious identity of the community. The "feet" rested on the Tegharza and Taoudenni salt mines, while subsidiary towns such as San, Sofala and Mopti, the storage and sorting centers of goods from the various provinces of the empire, were the neck, arms and legs. This model worked fairly well up to the rise of European colonialism and to this day is valid to a certain degree: although they are in decline, the port cities along the middle section of the Niger are still vital and have retained their strong character and originality. Salt still plays a major role in the economy of Timbuktu, the hub of camel and dugout traffic; the activities of salt extraction, transport and sale call for a great number of laborers, vendors and service suppliers, which is by no means an insignificant contribution to the development of a region on the fringes of the modern global market.

The Niger epitomizes the historical continuity of this huge slice of Africa, and the material well being of millions of people still depends on this river. Even during the worst cases of drought, the river continues to flow, which is quite a feat considering the fact that it makes the round trip journey in the desert virtually without any help: only two large tributaries, the Bani and Bénoué, flow into its middle and lower sections. Indeed, huge areas of its basin, which theoretically covers a surface area of over 800,000 sq. miles (2 million sq. km), are unserviceable, paralysed. The entire Sahara section, afflicted by thousands of years of continuous aridity, is a mere web of dry rivers and the waterway networks that radiate from the Adrar des Iforas, Atakor and Air mountains are totally disorganized. Heaps of sand cover the Tilemsi and Azaouak river valleys, which were once major tributaries of the Niger and are now almost unrecognizable; only the last section of the Dallol

116 top and 116-117 The barren landscape of the Sahara surrounds the large bend of the Niger River, which heads northward after the city of Ségou. In its journey across the desert the river has no affluents and proceeds among vast stretches of sand, its volume of water gradually decreasing. Since this region has no secure communication routes, the survival of the rare villages that spring up along the river banks depends on the river and caravan traffic.

116 bottom The life of these fishermen in the Djenné area of Mali is in keeping with ancient traditions, linked to the rhythm of the seasons and the whims of the great river.

117 bottom The villages in the inland delta of the Niger, in Mali, can be reached only by boat for most of the year. During the rainy season the river, made larger because of the rainfall on the Guinea Ridge, surrounds the village.

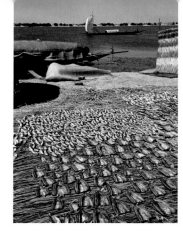

THE NIGER

118 top The fish caught in the Niger are thinly sliced or simply deprived of their entrails, dried in the sun, and then taken to the marketplace of Mopti.

118 center and bottom The traditional dugout, which is propelled by a long pole, is the most common means of transportation used in the inland delta of the Niger.

118-119 A fisherman casts his net in the waters of the Niger at Bamako. In the capital of Mali, which now has a population of four million, work opportunities are few and far between and people resort to traditional trades in order to survive.

Bosso takes in the seasonal but limited flood waters every so often.

The Niger manages to survive thanks to its fortunate "infancy." Its sources are situated in the rainiest area of the Guinea Ridge between the eastern slopes of the Fouta Djallon plateau and the Nimba Mts. Despite the low average altitude of about 1650 ft (500 m), these hills are subject to rainfall from the Atlantic for eight months a year, with hardly any seasonal variations. The Milo, Tinkisso, Niandan and Sankarani provide the Niger with an abundant and constant supply of water. At Siguiri, where the river leaves the highlands of Guinea, its outflow is twice that of the Senegal River. With the name of Djoliba, the Niger flows majestically toward Kourossa and the alluvial plain that leads to Bamako, the capital of Mali. After the rapids of Sotuba, the inclination of the Niger decreases gradually and is imperceptible near Ségou, where it begins to flow lazily in the huge tectonic basin that houses its inland delta. For the next 125 miles (200 km) the river has a gradient (fall) of only 33 ft (10 m), about one-fourth the gradient of the Nile before it empties into the sea. But the Niger is still 1240 miles (2000 km) from the ocean and must face its greatest difficulties: it is virtually without tributaries until Mopti, where it receives the waters of the Bani, and rainfall is rare indeed. Moreover, the flat terrain forces the river to move very slowly; the seasonal increase in outflow, which in the upper basin reaches its maximum in September-October, arrives at Mopti in November, Timbuktu in December and Niamey only in February, six months later. After Niamey the rainfall increases progressively, so that the high water period continues on into late spring. Then, again in September, the inflow of the Bénoué re-establishes the equilibrium, increasing the volume of the Niger to quite a degree.

In short, thanks to the rainfall in Guinea the river is never very low and has a rather regular regimen all year long. For a long time this unusual behavior – which is characterized by two high-water swells in the same period, but at a distance of thousands of miles – seemed to support the theory that the upper and lower Niger were two distinct rivers. The first maps show a totally imaginary course in which the river is connected to the Senegal or the Nile and yet empties into Lake Chad. For a certain period people even thought the Niger was connected with the Congo. In 1795, the British explorer Mungo Park discovered the river flowed from West to East, but the location of the mouth remained clouded in mystery. Park's following expedition, an attempt at going down from Ségou, ended in tragedy. Only thirty-six years later, the Lander brothers

119 bottom The Bani River, an affluent of the Niger, washes the walls of the ancient town of Djenné, in Mali. Founded around the year 800 on the east margin of the inland delta, this city was one of the hubs of the trade network that in the Middle Ages extended from the Mediterranean to the Gulf of Guinea.

THE NIGER

established that the basin of the Niger was a single body of water.

In its interminable course among the myriad canals of the inland delta, the Niger loses half its water through evaporation. The only permanent points of reference here are the hillocks with trees, many of which are dotted with the villages of the fishermen and farmers who live in this region. Some of the hillocks, called *togué*, are really burial mounds that were built from the 3rd century BC on by the ancient inhabitants, who grew rice and millet. On a level with Niafounké, massive strands of reddish sand dunes block the view of the horizon to the north. The river seems to come to a halt at this formidable obstacle, becoming an arc of parallel lakes in its patient search for an outlet. About 9,000 years ago the Niger strayed off in a vast basin in the central Sahara Desert, the so-called Araouane Lake; when and how it headed east and settled in its present

bed, is still a moot question among geologists. The alternation of wet and dry periods that created the configuration of the Sahara also influenced the evolution of the Niger River, which was continuously forced to react to the cyclical expansion and regression of the desert.

Between Timbuktu and Boureme the valley is straight and traverses barren and desolate land: only the hemispheric huts of the Tuareg sometimes dot the solitary and sandy shores. At the Tosaye gorges the Niger suddenly changes direction and heads toward Gao. One of the crucial battles in African history was fought in this zone, at Tondibi: in 1591, a few thousand Moroccan soldiers and Spanish mercenaries armed only with rifles managed to defeat the powerful army of Songhai, the last of the great empires of West Africa. Gao, the ancient capital of the kingdom, is now a dusty city with a few thousand inhabitants that is passing

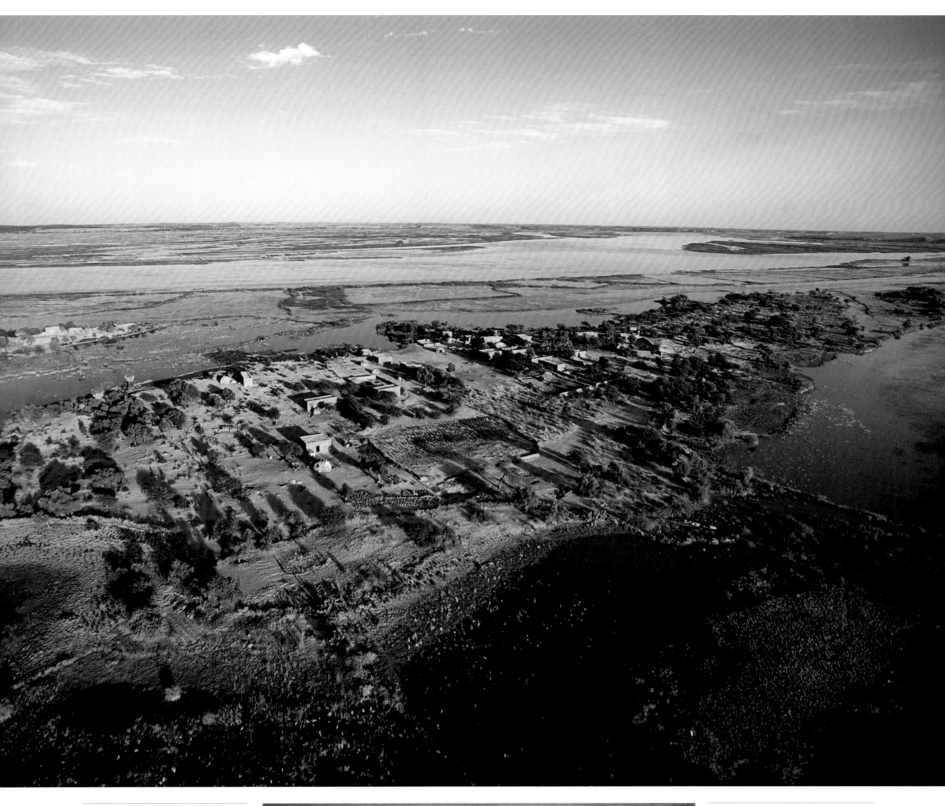

120 *Fishing and rice are the main resources for the inhabitants of the island villages that dot the course of the Niger above Gao. The apparently modest villages, which consist of a few low houses made of sun-dried clay, actually boast an illustrious past. Terra-cotta artifacts, grave goods of exquisite workmanship, and a large quantity of other archaeological objects clearly show that already in the 3rd century BC this region was the theater of a mysterious civilization.*

120-121 *Once out of the narrow Tosaye gorges the Niger widens as it enters the sandy plains that precede the city of Gao. Downstream from Bourem the river enters an extremely broad bed and its waters form a maze of channels interspersed with low islands.*

121 bottom *The villages of the Songhai farmers in the Gao area are made up of low houses with flat roofs, some with domes, built with sun-dried clay bricks plastered with mud.*

122 and 122-123 Large pink sand dunes flank the course of the Niger a few miles upstream from Gao, creating a fascinating contrast of lights and colors. The broad bend of the river in Mali is both an environmental and anthropological border, a region of transition between different worlds: the barrenness of the desert clashes with the thriving life in the steppes of the Sahel, tents are replaced by houses made of sun-dried clay, and dugouts take the place of dromedaries, in a land where contradiction is magically transformed into harmony.

*After taking in the large
inflow of water from the Bénoué
River and now in the plains of
southern Nigeria, the Niger
broadens in a vast bed that in
certain stretches is several miles
wide. The river proceeds slowly
and majestically toward its delta,*

*running down an almost
imperceptible gradient among large
sandbars and muddy islands. The
thick virgin forests that extend
beyond its shores comprise a
naturalist treasure trove, most of
which has yet to be explored by
scientists and researchers.*

THE NIGER

through a period of solitary stagnation and decline.

The river continues its descent, leaving behind the desert,
which gradually gives way to the steppes of the Sahel. For a
short stretch it marks the border between Niger and Benin, and
then washes the offshoots of the Atakora range, after which it
flows into Nigeria. The rapids of Aourou, where the roaring
Niger was once forced to pass through a passage no more than
33 ft (10 m) wide, are now swallowed up by a large artificial

lake created by the Kainji Dam. The clear waters of the Bénoué
flow into the Niger at Lokoja, merging with the water from the
Guinea delta. These two waterways, which are about the same
size, form a powerful river that after the city of Onitsha begins
to branch out into its second and final delta. The abundant
deposits of petroleum, which have been tapped since the late
1950s, make the Niger estuary the richest and most productive
region in Nigeria. Environmentalists agree with this description,
but for different reasons, since they are concerned about the
deterioration of the environment, which is threatening the
coastal forests of the Gulf of Biafra, the home of rare and
endangered species. There are no commercial harbors in the
Niger delta, as sand and silt block access for large boats.
Protected by an impenetrable mangrove jungle, the great
solitary river vanishes in the ocean.

124-125 Just before emptying into the Gulf of Biafra, the Niger splits up into a myriad of branches and channels, creating a vast fan-like configuration with a surface area of about 9650 sq. miles (25,000 sq. km). The petroleum extracted from the delta of the Niger is Nigeria's main economic resource.

125 bottom The rapids and falls that interrupt the course of the Niger before it merges with the Bénoué block navigation in the vicinity of the Niger-Nigerian frontier. The famous Bussa rapids, where the explorer Mungo Park died, are now submerged by an artificial lake.

CONGO
Kisangani
Mbandaka
Kingu
Brazzaville
PEOPLE'S
REPUBLIC OF
THE CONGO
Kinshasa

126-127 This view from a satellite shows the stretch of the Congo River near the Malebo Pool, where the river becomes a huge natural lake before plunging into the roaring Livingstone Rapids. In this photograph the large towns of Brazzaville (above) and Kinshasa (below) can be clearly seen.

THE CONGO

IN THE HEART OF AFRICA

"Going back up that river was like traveling backwards in time, to the dawn of the world, when plants grew freely on the Earth and the large trees were kings. A deserted waterway, a great silence and an impenetrable forest.

The air was hot, heavy, oppressive, stagnant. There was no joy in the brilliant sunlight. The long stretches of that river proceeded in solitary fashion, in the darkness of shaded distances." The words of Joseph Conrad are a fine description of the atmosphere of ominous mystery that pervaded the Congo River up to a little more than a century ago. In 1890, when Conrad took up service as a steamboat pilot in the Belgian Congo, the river had just been charted. Only 13 years earlier, an expedition headed by Stanley had gone down the Congo from Nyangwe to the Atlantic Ocean, finally shedding light on the geography of Central Africa and demonstrating that there was no link whatsoever between this river and the Nile system. Stanley's exploration of the rain forest, which lasted over a year, was fraught with difficulties: two-thirds of his men died from hardship and disease, or were killed during the continuous clashes with the native tribes.

Conrad's service lasted only four months but proved to be a crucial experience in the writer's life, and in his novel *Heart of Darkness* he called attention to the horrors of the would-be Free State of the Congo, which at the time was the personal property of King Leopold of Belgium and was subject to senseless and savage exploitation. Indeed, a stigma of mindless brutality seems to mark the entire history of this river, up to the present. Yet it was precisely on the estuary of the Congo that relations between Africa and Europe had their felicitous and promising beginning: the Portuguese, who had landed there in the late 1400s, initially had excellent relations with the local populations. The Kingdom of Kongo readily accepted Christianity and for a certain period had ambassadors in Lisbon. Then the slave trade suddenly interrupted this relationship among equals. The Congo sank into a period of anarchy and violence. Colonialism for its part left wounds that were difficult to heal. In that fragile land beset by heated tribal rivalry, national independence had

a hard lot: there were still many wars and massacres, in a spiral of violence that to this day looms over the humid area of the river and its tributaries like a pall.

Indeed, not much has changed along the Congo River since Conrad's time. The great forest, although no longer virgin land, continues to be a formidable obstacle for communications. Given the lack of roads and railways, the river is still the only reliable route between the ocean and the cities scattered in the boundless jungle that covers the Congo basin, a surface area of 1.4 million sq. miles (3.5 million sq. km).

The jungle has not always been the same size, since with time the alternation of wet and dry periods has greatly modified its magnitude. At times the vegetation receded so much that it clustered along the banks of the rivers, only to extend once again and cover large areas of the savanna. This phenomenon has had a crucial effect on the evolutionary processes. Shelter zones that have remained unchanged for thousands and thousands of years alternate with areas of more recent expansion, each characterized by different species, many of which are endemic, in a continuous flow and exchange from one habitat to the other.

The Congo is the main artery around which the various pieces of this extraordinary mosaic of ecosystems revolve. The river, about 2975 miles (4800 km) long, begins it long journey toward the Atlantic far from the shadowy and warm forest world, in a region of uniform savanna highlands. Its name also changes: its most important headstream, normally considered the upper Congo, is called the Lualaba River, which begins in the hills that mark the southern border of Shaba and flows directly northward, swift and sure of itself. The course of the Chambezi River, the twin of the former, is much more uncertain: after lingering for a long while in the plains of Zambia, it flows into the vaguely defined outlying areas of Lake Bangweulu, which during the rainy season becomes a huge marshland. When it has emerged from Lake Bangweulu, the Chambezi becomes the Luapula River, which continues for a few hundred miles and then flows into Lake Mweru. The Luvua River, the last part of this metamorphosis, merges with the Lualaba above Kongolo, which is where the

127 bottom Forests and immense marshes surround the middle course of the Congo, which at times branches out into a labyrinth of secondary channels whose configuration is constantly changing. "In that river you can be lost as if you were in a desert," wrote Joseph Conrad, who in the late 19th century worked as a steamboat pilot on the Congo.

Congo River proper begins its course. After the confluence
with the Lukuga River, which comes from Lake Tanganyika,
the Congo precipitates with a roar into a series of entrenched
gorges not more than 330 ft (100 m) wide, the so-called
Gates of Hell, the threshold of the forest.

At Nyangwe what was a clear sky is already filled with
fog and mist. The horizon is blocked in all directions by a
gloomy green veil. Nyangwe was for a long time the last
outpost of the Arab merchants, the center of the ivory and
slave trade, beyond which lay the unknown, a hostile world
without any known points of reference. The villages of Bantu
fishermen and farmers lie at the edge of the forest, an
uninhabitable environment for everyone save the pygmies,
who feel perfectly at home there. The Mbitu pygmies, a
population of about 40,000 people, live in the Ituri rain
forest, which extends east of Kisangani up to the great plains
that open out toward East Africa. Their economy is based on
hunting and gathering wild fruit, activities that involve the

entire community, including women and children. The forest
provides the Mbitu with everything they need for
subsistence, so that they have plenty of time for
entertainment and leisure. Far from being a mysterious and
dangerous place, this region is friendly and hospitable,
quite the opposite of the "dirty, dry" and treeless land that
delimits it.

Outside of the forest life is inconceivable. The
anthropologist Colin Turnbull, who studied the pygmy
society in Ituri for years, tells us that the outside world is a
totally alien system for these people. Turnbull took one of his
guides to the savannas of Virunga. The hunter's reaction to a
distant herd of buffaloes was one of indifference: "What
insects are those?" he asked. The anthropologists' efforts to
convince him that those black figures on the plain were large
herbivores that were very good to eat were in vain.
Perspective, that is, the evaluation of the relationship
between distance and size, was simply extraneous to the

THE CONGO

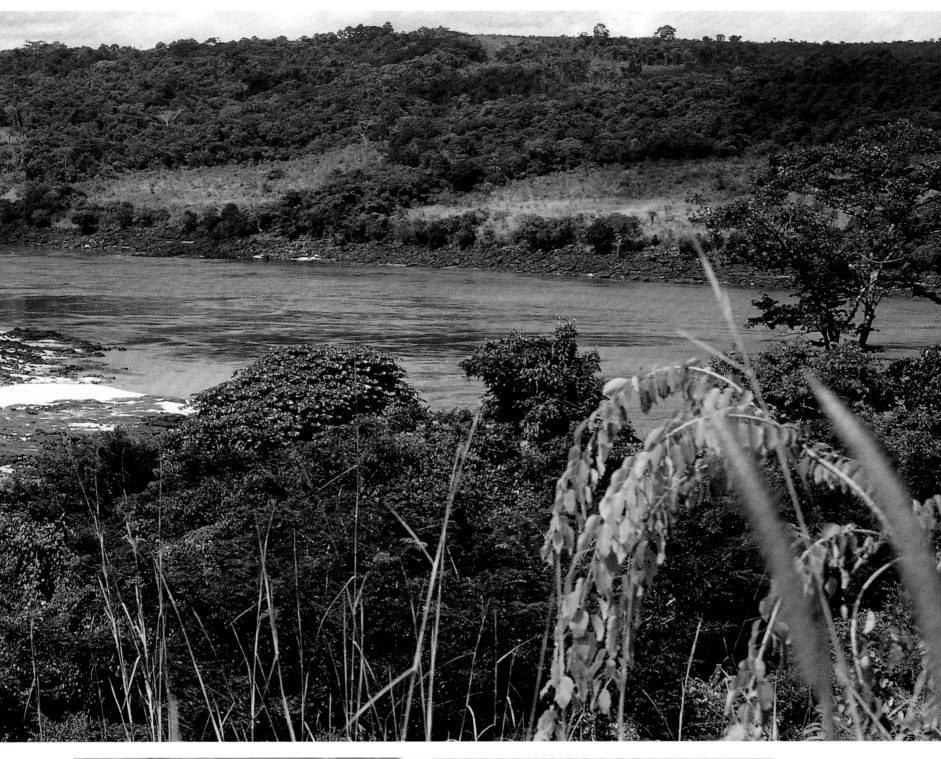

129 bottom Once out of Malebo Pool, where it becomes 14 miles (23 km) wide, the Congo proceeds for a short stretch through an unspoiled landscape. The gloomy forest that flanks the river for most of its middle course is replaced by less dense vegetation. The cities of Kinshasa and Brazzaville are a short distance downstream.

128-129 The Congo River flows calmly in the area of the capital city of Brazzaville. The course of the river was explored at the end of the 19th century by a French aristocrat of Italian origin, Pierre de Brazza, who managed to procure a great deal of territory for France without resorting to violence. Brazzaville was named after him.

hunter's perceptive system, which was based on the needs of life in the forest, where visibility is limited to a few feet.

Enlarged by all its tributaries, the Congo River is now a powerful river that flows in a vast bed with rather vague boundaries, creating a maze of islets and secondary canals. The Boyoma rapids below Ubundu suddenly interrupt the placid course: for 62 miles (100 km) the river runs over a rocky bed, precipitating in a series of rapids. Only the Wagenia fishermen dare face the current in their dugouts to place their large conical fish pots in the frothy water. The Wagenia cataract marks the beginning of the middle section of the Congo, which flows majestically toward Kisangani.

A steamboat connects this city and the port of Kinshasa; the voyage may take from eight to twelve days if no unexpected circumstance interrupts the navigation, which is already made difficult by the sandbars and the sudden changes in the conditions of the river. The ship is a means of transport, a floating marketplace-hospital-post office-café in one, a meeting place, and whatever else the backwash of progress may gradually bring to these isolated regions. Game, piles of dried fish, live animals, palm oil, agricultural produce and all kinds of merchandise are heaped helter-skelter on the bridge of the barges, which are always surrounded by swarms of dugouts waiting to return to the villages loaded with the

THE CONGO

131 center and bottom The technique used by the Wagenia fishermen at the Boyoma Falls, near Kisangani, is singular, to say the least, and certainly risky. The bamboo scaffolds built at the bottom of the most violent rapids are used as platforms from which large conical fish pots are set in the water with their open ends facing upstream. The fish are pushed by the current into the pots and are then hauled ashore. This apparently simple maneuver requires great skill, equilibrium and courage.

130-131 Having lived for centuries on the banks of the Congo upstream from Kisangani, the Wagenia tribe fishermen are not daunted by the violence of the Boyoma Falls, which were formerly named after Stanley. This famous explorer visited the area in 1877 and in his travel journal described their method of fishing with large fish pots, which he found was quite efficient.

131 top The pirogue or dugout canoe, propelled by a long pole or with the aid of a paddle, is the only means of transport for those living in the middle course of the Congo, an area totally without any infrastructure. At times these boats are quite rudimentary — tree trunks hollowed with an ax.

132-133 and 133 bottom The
humidity that emerges every day
from the jungle is sometimes
transformed into fog so thick that
it blocks navigation even for the
large ships that run between
Kinshasa and Kisangani.

133 top A consignment of high-
quality wood goes down the Congo
toward the port of Kinshasa. The
commercial exploitation of the large
rain forests that cover most of the
Congo basin is blocked by the lack
of means of transportation.

THE CONGO

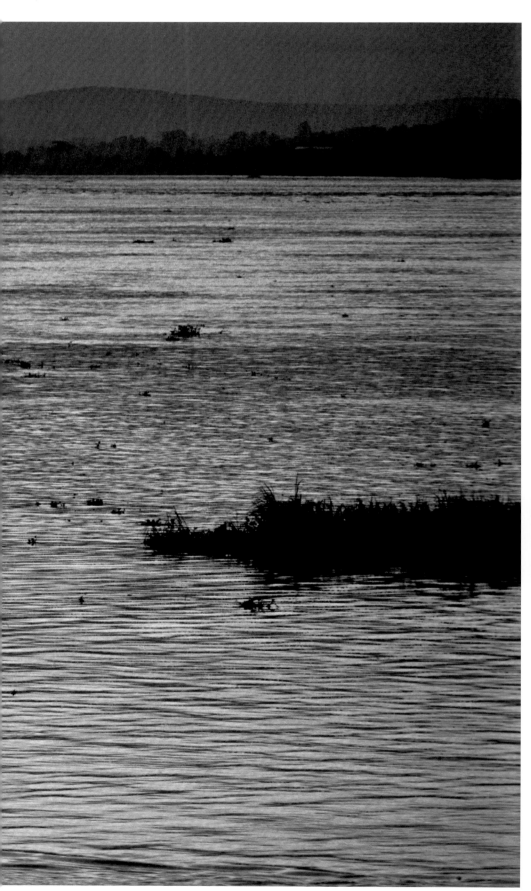

precious consumer goods from the estuary cities.

The Congo, which in certain places is 9.3 miles (15 km) wide, is not subject to floods or low water. Thanks to its geographic position bridging the Equator, it is always fed constantly by its tributaries: in keeping with the symmetrical alternation of rainy seasons, the water flow of the tributaries from the north and south compensate one another, and so the Congo is abundant and torrential all year long.

The Ubangi, which is the major tributary, flows into the Congo at Mbandaka, the only town of any importance before Kinshasa and Brazzaville. After the Congo merges with the Kasai the forest becomes less thick and the limestone Crystal Mts. appear on the horizon. Embanked by this barrier, the river becomes a vast lake about 12.5 miles (20 km) wide and 20 miles (32 km) long: the so-called Malebo Pool, once called the Stanley Pool.

The Livingstone Rapids suddenly begin here in a series of

cataracts of unspeakable violence whose fury is placated only at Matadi. Embedded in the deep gorge between the mountains, the Congo lashes out with all its power in this interminable narrow passage, which for four centuries was the main obstacle for the exploration and exploitation of the interior.

From Matadi to the Atlantic the river flows quietly among flooded mangrove forests and palm groves: nothing seems to have remained of the powerful Congo except an immense stretch of muddy water agitated by the ocean waves. But in the depths of the ocean the current is quiet. The force of the Congo River dies out in this unknown abyss and is now invisible, a stranger to itself and extraneous to human events.

THE ZAMBESI
A WILD PARADISE

Livingstone came within sight of the Zambesi River for the first time in early August 1851, near the city of Sesheke, on the present-day Zambia-Namibia border. This was a fatal encounter. From that time on the great explorer was plagued by a vision: that massive river was the providential path that would open the heart of Africa to the Christian faith and progress. Not even the rumors of large waterfalls eighty miles below this point shook his certainty and determination. Thus, tracing the course of the Zambesi became a necessity, even a duty, for Livingstone. For the following twelve years the river was an obsession, which ended in total and definitive failure. Livingstone traveled up and down the Zambesi, following its course on foot, in a dugout canoe and with all the other available means, from Mozambique to Angola. He discovered what he patriotically named the Victoria Falls, carefully explored the territory that stretched as far as the eye could see beyond the marshy shores, and went up the Shire, the last large tributary to the north. Curiously enough, despite his mania Livingstone never attempted to reach the source of the river, even though he came close to it during his trek toward Luanda. And, what is more important, he did not spot the rapids of Cabora Bassa, which shattered his hopes.

The Zambesi rises in northwestern Zambia, in the Katanga highlands, which mark the divide with the Congo River basin.

There are no mountains or mysterious jungles that conceal the origin of the fourth longest river in Africa: whoever wants to take a walk in the brush can easily reach the spring of clear water where the Zambesi begins its long journey to the Indian Ocean. Almost at once the river enters Angola, then re-emerges in Zambia at the Chavuma district where it becomes a series of modest rapids.

Only five bridges cross over the Zambesi in its 1717-mile (2770-km) course. The first one is situated a short distance after the border, at Chinyingi: a footbridge 660 ft (200 m) long held up by a network of steel cables and tension rods. It was built by Capuchin missionaries from the area about twenty years ago, after the ferry accident in which four of their colleagues were killed. Below Chinyingi is an absolutely flat plain covered with grass and forests, where the roads are nothing more than faint tracks in the sand and the presence of humans is only occasional.

Within the vague confines of the national parks and reserves that border the right-hand or southern side of the river, the old, wild and virgin Africa of travel books appears in all its primeval magnificence. In keeping with the seasons, large herds of elephants, buffaloes and antelopes travel in search of water and grazing land, followed by hosts of predators. Everything seems to be immutable, as eternal as the silence of the night, which is interrupted every so often by the wheezing of the hippopotami. The Upper Zambesi region is one of the most 'backward' in southern Africa: communication is difficult, the social and educational infrastructures are virtually non-existent, and the public hospitals are generally inadequate for the needs of the population. Until Zambia became an independent nation in the early 1960s, most of this territory, formerly known as Barotseland, was part of the Lozi kingdom, whose king, the *Litunga*, still wields considerable power. However, the monarchist sympathies of the Lozi population did not please the new government of Lusaka, which excluded the provinces of the upper Zambesi region from the country's economic development projects.

It is the river, with its high and low water levels, which marks the rhythm of life in remote Barotseland. It not only

134 bottom With its huge mouth wide open, a hippopotamus suddenly emerges from the waters of the Zambesi River. These creatures, which can easily be 11 ft (3.5 m) long and weigh up to three tons, may become very aggressive if they are disturbed or threatened by humans.

134-135 and 135 bottom Elephants and lions are a common sight in the large national parks that lie along the upper and middle course of the Zambesi. A particularly interesting protected area is Mana Pools, situated in the alluvial plains of northern Zimbabwe, below Lake Kariba.

136 top and 137 bottom Downstream from Victoria Falls, the Zambesi in certain stretches is 1.2 miles (2 km) wide. While up to this point it headed south toward the inland Okavango delta, it now flows eastward, following the crevices in the terrain resulting from the tectonic movements that created the Great Rift Valley.

136 bottom The climate and quality of the soil determine the various types of flora that grow along the banks of the Zambesi. The sandy and alluvial terrain hosts palm groves and luxuriant vegetation, while the predominant plants in the rocky zones are baobab and the species typical of the Kalahari brush.

136-137 Flowing between tall basalt faces, the Zambesi precipitates thunderously down the deep and inaccessible Batoka gorges. In this crevice, sometimes less than 65 ft (20 m) wide, the river twists its way through a series of extremely violent rapids, marking extremely steep gradients in only a few miles of its course.

provides the Lozi with abundant fish and water for irrigation, but also determines the quality of the settlements. Every year, thanks to the heavy rains, the Zambesi flows over its banks and into the plain, which becomes an immense lake. In April the heartland of the Lozi, with a surface area of over 2800 sq. miles (7000 sq. km.) from Mongu to the Angolan border, lies under 6.6 ft (2 m) of silty water. This is when the royal drums beat to announce that the moment has come for the *kuomboka*, the ceremony that marks the move of the royal court from the summer residence in Lealui to the palace in Limulunga, about 12.5 miles (20 km) away on the low hills along the east shore of the river. The *Litunga*, followed by a procession of dignitaries, sits on the *Nalikwanda*, the enormous royal dugout

that will take him to his other residence. The boat, crowned by a large papier-mâché elephant, is propelled by 120 expert rowers wearing traditional costumes. The landing at Limulunga, just before sunset, is greeted by a large, festive crowd. The king appears before his subjects dressed in a black and gold ceremonial uniform, with a bicorn decorated with a tuft of white ostrich feathers. The uniform, along with cases of glass beads, was donated to the *Litunga* of the time by Cecil Rhodes; in exchange, the English were granted the right to exploit the mineral resources of the region as they wished.

The Zambesi proceeds southward through the lowlands of Barotseland, where its bed is 1.85 miles (3 km) wide in some stretches. As it approaches the Namibian border, its course

138 A cloud of mist always
envelops the Victoria Falls gorge,
which is surrounded by a rain
forest. The locals call the falls
"Thundering Smoke," but the
original inhabitants of this area
christened them Shongwe, or "Place
of the Rainbow."

138-139 Viewed from above,
Victoria Falls reveal all their
extraordinary power, especially
during the dry season, when the
characteristic mist is less dense and
allows one to spot the basalt shelf
from which the Zambesi plunges
into the chasm below.

THE ZAMBESI

becomes more capricious and is often interrupted by rapids and small falls. At Sesheke it suddenly changes direction, heading east. Millions of years ago the Zambesi flowed into the vast inland sea that lay in the middle of Botswana. Then the huge crevices created by the tectonic movement that created the Great Rift Valley channeled it into its present bed. The same thing occurred with the Kwando River, which under the name of Chobe empties into the Zambesi at Kasane. A short distance from here, the river precipitates with a deafening roar into Victoria Falls. The mist that always envelops the falls can be seen from 25 miles (40 km) away. The indigenous populations called the falls *Mosi-oa-Tunya*, or Thundering Smoke. It was the ubiquitous Livingstone who gave them the name of his queen. On 15 November 1855 he stood at the edge of the abyss on the islet of Kazeruka and recorded his impression: "Crawling terrorized at the tip of the island, I saw below me an enormous gorge between one bank

and the other of the Zambesi River; a mass of water 2540 ft to 3000 ft (800 – 1000 m) wide was falling from a height of 110 ft (33 m) and bubbling and frothing in an abyss 50 ft (15 m) wide." His estimates were completely wrong: the Victoria Falls are about 1.05 miles (roughly 1.7 km) wide, while the chasm is about 360 ft (110 m) deep and 198 ft (60 m) wide. The Zambesi casts 17.7 million gallons (68 million liters) of water per minute into that chasm, a quantity that may increase tenfold during the rainy season. When he returned to England, Livingstone had to withstand the complaints of his publisher, who said that the explorer's description contained too few adjectives for a bestseller. So they decided to invent a series of high-sounding phrases that included angels in flight, triple rainbows and "a myriad liquid comets." We do not know how much of this ridiculous literary padding was created by Livingstone himself, but in any case he got rich with the publication of his memoirs.

The mist that rises ceaselessly from the falls has produced an authentic rain forest, complete with primitive ferns and orchids. Monkeys and birds with brightly colored plumage abound in this natural park, a luxuriant belt that is in marked contrast with the ocean of brush that covers the highlands of Zimbabwe and Zambia. During the dry season, when the clouds of mist become thinner, one can catch sight of the basalt shelf from which the Zambesi plunges into the chasm. Basalt is very resistant to erosion but here has fractures that are perpendicular to the course of the river, and the Zambesi flowed precisely in these 'weak points': the Batoka gorges, which extend for about 62 miles (100 km) from the falls, are the result of this implacable erosion. Only 10,000 years ago Victoria Falls was pushed quite a way eastward, and this process of recession is still underway. Inch by inch, the Zambesi River is opening a new passage through the Devil's Cataract, at the beginning of the canyon.

Once out of the entrenched course of the Batoka highlands, the river goes on its way, sometimes animated by rapids, until it flows into the artificial Lake Kariba. After a series of seemingly insurmountable difficulties, the Kariba Dam was finished in 1960 by a group of Italian firms. Its power plant provides Zambia and Zimbabwe with much of their electric power. Between Kariba and Kanyemba, at the Mozambique border, the Zambesi River flows freely through a desolate,

139 bottom In this aerial view of Victoria Falls one can see, from left to right, the Devil's Cataract, the Main Falls and Rainbow Falls, which are separated by the promontory of Kazeruka Island. The Main Falls are 2800 ft (850 m) wide and their volume of water remains constant throughout the year.

140-141 As it enters Mozambique the Zambesi penetrates a series of deep gorges and then flows broadly into the large artificial basin of Cabora Bassa. According to legend, in the depths of the lake are the mysterious silver mines of Chicova, which were exploited by the Portuguese as long ago as the 1600s.

140 bottom The railway bridge of Muturara, situated halfway between the city of Tete and the Indian Ocean coast, is one of the few that cross over the Zambesi River. The railway links the port of Beira and the rich mining areas that lie around Tete.

THE ZAMBESI

141 top Viewed from the Kariba dam, which regulates its flow, the Zambesi appears to have lost its former power and majesty. The artificial lake which extends over 1930 sq. miles (5000 sq. km) and provides both Zambia and Zimbabwe with electric power.

141 bottom The city of Tete, an old Portuguese outpost, the Zambesi proceeds peacefully through land that has remained unchanged over the centuries. In the vicinity of the town of Muturara, after taking in the abundant waters of the Shire, the river heads slowly toward the Indian Ocean.

uninhabited region: malaria and trypanosomiasis, or sleeping sickness, transmitted by the tsetse fly, discourage the creation of permanent settlements, so that the land is the domain of wild animals. In this section the river takes in the waters of two major tributaries, the Kafur and the Luangwa, which increase its size considerably. Until 1974 its entry into Mozambique was heralded by the Cabora Bassa rapids, which are now submerged in the large man-made basin. As the Zambesi approaches the labyrinthine delta at the Indian Ocean, it becomes broader and more majestic. Here the Shire River empties into it from the north, carrying the waters of Lake Malawi.

Since the mid-16th century, when the first Portuguese adventurers founded the trading posts of Sena and Tete, the Zambesi River has remained basically the same: wild and unpredictable.

ASIA

With a surface area of 16,833,000 sq. miles (43,608,000 sq. km), Asia is the largest continent on Earth. Despite this, its rivers are generally shorter than those in the other continents (though there are notable exceptions) and their drainage area is smaller. This depends mostly on the physical configuration of Asia, the middle section of which is occupied by vast desert lakes bordered by mountain ranges. The few rivers that cross the Gobi and Takla Makan deserts disappear in the sand since they have no outlet to the sea. West of the Pamirs, in the arid steppes of Turkestan, the Syr Darya and Amu Darya rivers end in Lake Aral, which is now the almost dry 'carcass' of an ancient inland sea. All the large Asian rivers (except for the Amur) that empty in the Indian and Pacific Ocean originate in the Tibetan plateau north of the Himalayas.

The Ganges, Indus, Brahmaputra, Mekong, Salween and the rivers of China, all flow – at least at the beginning of their course – from east to west, following the alignment of the mountain chains. Some run for long stretches in parallel valleys: this is particularly true of the Mekong, Salween and Yangtze, which in north Yunnan almost touch one another and are separated by narrow dividing ranges. The average discharge varies considerably according to the configuration of the delta, the amount of monsoon rainfall, and the water from thaws, so that it ranges from 625,000 cubic ft (25,000 cubic m) per second for the Brahmaputra to the 62,500 cubic ft (2,500 cubic m) of the Yellow River (but the outflow of this latter can increase tenfold during the high-water season). There is always a great amount of silt deposit, which in thousands of years has created some of the most fertile plains on Earth, where most of the Asian population lives.

The rivers that flow into the Arctic Ocean have different characteristics: they cross through regions with small populations where the towns are rare and the cold climate makes almost any form of agriculture impossible. The Yenisei, Lena and Ob rise up from southern ranges of the Siberian plateau, which extend from the Altai Mts. along the Mongolian border to the Stanovoi Range. They are blocked by the ice for most of the year, and are therefore navigable only in summer, but their colossal hydroelectric potential is destined to play a decisive role in the development of the so-called virgin lands of eastern Russia.

The third waterway center of Asia, the Armenian plateau, is in Turkey: this is point of origin of the only two large rivers in the Middle East, The Tigris and Euphrates. Together with the Yellow River and the Indus, they were the vital sap of some of the most ancient civilizations in the history of mankind.

142 left Rice paddies in the Mekong River delta near Vung Tau, South Vietnam.

142 center The Brahmaputra flowing through the plateau of Tibet.

142 right Boats moving along the shores of the Ganges at Varanasi, India.

143 A stretch of the Huang He at the city of Zhengzhou, in Henan Province, China.

144-145 An endless strip of vegetation marks the passage of the Euphrates through the town of Kemah, downstream from Erzincan. The river, which at this point is called the Firat, crosses the barren regions of eastern Turkey, the cradle of civilization in very ancient times.

145 top This torrent running through the snow-capped mountains of eastern Turkey marks the beginning of the Euphrates River. The inflow from other waterways that descend from the region north of Erzurum give rise to one of the most important rivers in the Middle East.

145 bottom The clear blue sky in eastern Turkey is mirrored in the waters of the Euphrates. This river, which by the end of summer has very little water, is at its maximum discharge in spring, when it reaches the top of the arches of this bridge.

THE TIGRIS AND EUPHRATES

THE FASCINATION OF THE PAST

The first known world map dates from 2500 years ago and was carved on a clay tablet a little larger than a pack of cigarettes. The Earth is represented with disarming simplicity: it appears as a flat disk surrounded by water and traversed by two parallel lines that depict the shores of the Euphrates River. In the middle of the circle, surrounded by satellite cities, is Babylon, the most famous urban area in antiquity. Actually, the Babylonians were truly excellent astronomers who were able to calculate almost perfectly the orbits of the moon and the movements of the stars. This map was not intended as a means of transmitting geographic information, but as a precise symbolic message: Babylon is the center of the world.

It was in fact in Mesopotamia, the Greek word for the "land between rivers," that one of the most extraordinary adventures in human civilization began 7000 years ago in the heart of that Fertile Crescent whose arc extended up to Palestine and Sinai. This was the cradle of our culture, law, philosophy, science and art. The first form of writing grew up in Mesopotamia and gradually evolved from pictographic writing to the abstract cuneiform script. It was here that the 12-month calendar, 60-minute hour, and the basics of algebra, geometry and medicine were created. The eclipses were predicted with great accuracy and the duration of the solar year was calculated with a margin of error of only 4 minutes and 32 seconds. The first code of laws was drawn up by Hammurabi on the shores of the Euphrates around 1800 BC.

That strip of land between the twin rivers was the birthplace of metallurgy and agriculture, which thanks to sophisticated irrigation techniques became a permanent and profitable activity that fed a large urban population. The foundation of the cities of Erech, Eridu, Ur, Nippur and Adab dates from the IVth millennium BC, and the first Mesopotamian empire, established at Akkad, achieved its apogee 1500 years before the birth of Rome. After the decline of Ur, wars and invasions forged Babylon, which was destroyed and rebuilt several times and for ten centuries was the political and cultural capital of the region.

In the meantime, in the north, the banks of the Tigris (to the east of the Euphrates) witnessed the rise of the Assyrians, whose military power was based on their war chariots and iron weapons: in a short time their dominion, which began in 900 BC, extended from the Persian Gulf to Egypt. In the following centuries the Medes, Scythians, Chaldaeans and then the

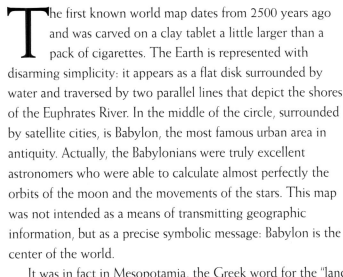

Persians vied for dominion in the land between the two rivers. Alexander the Great dreamed of Babylon as the capital of a world empire, but he died there in 323 BC. The death of the Macedonian conqueror was the ideal conclusion of the most ancient chapter of an age-old story that was often bloody but was always marked by creative genius.

Properly speaking, Mesopotamia is mostly situated within the confines of modern-day Iraq, delimited to the east by the last section of the Iranian plateau and to the west by the desert tableland of Saudi Arabia and Syria. The climate is dry, with temperatures of up to 50° C in the summer, and the rainfall is scarce and irregular. Mesopotamia owes its fortune exclusively to the Tigris and Euphrates, which for millennia deposited a thick

layer of silt on the sterile plain, creating a gigantic oasis of fertile land in an environment that is hostile to human endeavor. Today as in the past, the lives of millions of people depend on the seasonal floods and the utilization of the water to irrigate the fields.

The Tigris and Euphrates both rise in Turkey, in the mountains of the Armenian plateau. Initially they follow an almost parallel course and then diverge, approaching each other near Baghdad, where the two rivers are barely 218 miles (353 km) apart. Lastly, at Qurnah the Tigris flows into the Euphrates to form the Shatt al-Arab, which empties into the Persian Gulf. The drainage basin of the Tigris-Euphrates system covers about 300,000 sq. miles (750,000 sq. km), extending over vast regions of Turkey, Syria and Iraq. The headwaters of the 1674-mile (2700-km) long Euphrates are situated in the barren mountainous area north of Erzurum, at an altitude of over 9900 ft (3000 m). At first the river is called Kara Su, then it takes the name of Firat as it is entrenched in a deep, narrow valley.

146-147 The colossal Atatürk Dam, which is the largest in Turkey, takes in 80% of the water in the Euphrates, providing most of the country's electric power. However, the containment of the upper course of the river may seriously damage the economy of Syria and Iraq.

146 bottom Mute witnesses of history, these imposing ruins of a citadel dominate the course of the Euphrates. Many of the castles and fortresses in Syria were built in the period of the Crusades.

147 top After leaving behind the mountains of Turkey, the Euphrates flows into the vast, rather flat semi-desert so typical of Syria and Iraq.

147 center The contrast between
the surrounding arid regions and
the areas washed by the Euphrates
is striking: palm groves and
vegetable gardens, cities and
villages alike owe their existence to
the uninterrupted flow of this great
river.

147 bottom Founded in the 3rd
century BC during the reign of the
Seleucid dynasty, the stronghold of
Dura-Europos overlooks the
Euphrates Valley. For five
centuries this city was one of the
most prosperous trade centers in
Syria.

THE EUPHRATES

During its course it receives the waters of several tributaries that in spring swell as they receive the melted snow. After Keban, where it takes in the large amount of water from the Murad, the rushing flow of the river is checked by a series of large dams and it runs through the barren edges of the Anti-Taurus Mts. and into a huge greenish-blue lake. The Turkish government's medium-term development project calls for the construction of about twenty dams on the upper sections of the Euphrates and Tigris. The advantages for Turkey are clear, but the completed project may seriously jeopardize the economy of Syria and Iraq, whose water supply would be halved.

The Euphrates River leaves the Taurus Mts. behind and suddenly turns southward, entering the plain of Syria. At this point it is close to the Mediterranean, only 93 miles (150 km) away, and quite far from the Tigris River. This steppe region, which is not so arid and has a good supply of underground water, was once traversed by one of the very ancient trade routes that linked the Mesopotamian cities and the coast of Lebanon, Anatolia and Armenia, sources of precious materials such as copper, silver and construction wood. The focal point of this trade was the city of Mari, which the Euphrates touches before the Iraqi border. The Sumerians, the rulers of Akkad and the Assyrian Empire all wanted to conquer Mari for its riches, but the city always managed to retain a certain degree of independence until it was destroyed by Hammurabi in 1759 BC. Among the ruins of its labyrinthine royal palace, which had no less than 260 rooms, archaeologists found over 20,000 clay tablets with cuneiform inscriptions: a precious archive that offers a lively description of the city's everyday life and historic events.

When it arrives at Baghdad, the Euphrates, now several hundred feet wide and linked to the Tigris via an artificial canal, heads southward toward Babylon and southern Mesopotamia. Enclosed by tall embankments, the river moves into a completely horizontal plain as the valley flattens out,

and the Euphrates, which in some sections has an elevated bed, meanders broadly, branching out into secondary arms often obstructed by the accumulation of sediment. In the past the river followed a different course and its banks touched the walls of Ur, which are now surrounded by a desert of dry mud. The canals that once carried water to the cultivated fields dried up and the city was abandoned for good in the 4th century BC. The riches and fame of Ur, the fabulous treasures of gold and precious stones found in the gloomy tombs of the kings, all depended totally on the generosity of the Euphrates.

THE TIGRIS

148 top The Tigris winds its way in a deep and narrow valley through the mountains of Turkish Kurdistan, where there are many rapids and small waterfalls, so that the river is torrential up to the city of Mosul, Iraq.

148 bottom left Flowing placidly in its wide bed in the plains of Iraq, the Tigris heads south with an almost imperceptible gradient. The waters of this river, which are regulated by canals, have been used for irrigation since the 3rd century BC.

148 bottom right The tortuous course of the Tigris splits the city of Baghdad, which was founded in AD 762 by the Abbasids near the ruins of ancient Ctesiphon. In the vicinity of the capital of Iraq the Tigris and Euphrates are only 18.5 miles (30 km) apart.

149 Fog banks, sandbars and brackish lagoons characterize the coastline of the Persian Gulf at a level with the delta of the Shatt al-Arab, the large navigable waterway formed by the merger of the Tigris and Euphrates.

The Tigris, on the other hand, seems to have played a minor role in the rise of Sumerian civilization. Although it is not as long as the Euphrates, its outflow is twice as large and in its lower section it is surrounded by vast marshy zones unfit for human habitation. Furthermore, the river flows in an entrenched bed in the plain, which makes it impossible to utilize the water for irrigation by exploiting the force of gravity. The Tigris, known as the Hiddikel in the Bible, rises at Lake Hazar in the Armenian Taurus Mts., northwest of the city of Diyarbekir. Interrupted by rapids and falls, it begins its journey among the mountains of eastern Turkey and up to the Syrian border, which it skirts for about 19 miles (30 km). Once in Iraq, the Tigris meanders rather slowly; when it reaches Mosul it is already a full-fledged river. Those undulating plains that descend softly toward the banks of the Tigris were the birthplace of Assyrian civilization. It was here that Nineveh and Nimrud, the cities of Sennacherib and Ashurbanipal, rose up as the capitals of the first large empire in the

Middle East. The impressive ruins of the buildings and fortifications, the stone lions, the human figures with wings and eagles' heads, bear witness to the splendor of a culture that was at once warlike and highly sophisticated.

From Mosul to Baghdad the Tigris River flows sluggishly southward in a broad valley. In this section it receives four major tributaries that come from the mountains of Iran and Kurdistan: the Little Zab, the Great Zab, the Adhaim and the Diyala, which are responsible for the ruinous spring floods. When the river reaches the city of Al-Kut the landscape changes drastically and the plain becomes an expanse of pools, canals and dry riverbeds that absorb 80 percent of its water. At the confluence with the Euphrates, after flowing for 10545 miles (1700 km), the Tigris, no more than 198 ft (60 m) wide, looks like a secondary tributary of its big brother. The two rivers merge at Shatt al-Arab, the great waterway that marks the border with Iran. The Persian Gulf, known in Babylonian cosmogony as the Bitter River, is only 111 miles (180 km) away.

THE BRAHMAPUTRA

THE SON OF BRAHMA

One day Brahma, the god who created the Universe, decided to spread his seed over the Earth in order to benefit all mankind. For the act of conception he chose a woman called Amogha, the wife of the venerable Shantanu, considered the wisest of the wise men. When Amogha gave birth, Shantanu was struck with divine inspiration and decided the take the child beyond the great mountain barrier, onto the barren highland dominated by Mt. Kailas, the famed sacred mountain. Here a miracle took place and the newborn

child was transformed into water, a gigantic expanse of cool currents that flowed onto the Earth. The *Kalika Purana*, a 10th-century Indian text, gives this explanation for the origin of the Brahmaputra, or "son of Brahma," the 'male' river *par excellence*.

In this case legend and reality coincide perfectly. The headstreams of the Brahamputra lie in the glaciers of Kubi Gangri, about 16,500 ft (5000 m) above sea level, in the remote region of western Tibet between the Himalayas and Mt. Kailas. That maze of ridges and valleys goes to make up the divide where some of the largest rivers in South Asia begin – from the Indus to the Ganges. But while the Ganges soon moves away from the mountains and flows in the large plains of northern India, the Indus and Brahmaputra linger for a great distance in the craggy, solitary valleys, skirting in opposite directions the north slopes of the Himalaya range. This highly important mountain complex, which is to this day hard to penetrate, appeared on maps only in the early 20th century thanks to the journeys of Sven Hedin. On 10 September 1907, at his camp on the slopes of Mt. Kailas, the Swedish explorer could finally celebrate the success of his long treks on the Tibetan plateau: "At last I experienced the joy," he wrote in his diary, "of being the first white man to reach the headstreams of the Indus and the Brahmaputra, two rivers that have been famous since time immemorial, which encircle the entire Himalaya range like the chelae of a crab." The comparison is perfect: while the Indus heads westward, burrowing its way among the giants of the Karakorum range and the last spurs of the Nanga Parbat peak, the Brahmaputra flows almost immediately into a broad valley the passes eastward through southern Tibet for over 745 miles (1200 km).

In this long and almost straight stretch in Tibetan territory, the river is called the Tsang-po. It flows in a vast sandy bed, breaking up into a large number of branches that separate and merge in continuation, carrying with them an enormous

150 *An enormous glacier formed by the snows of Kubi Gangri and Mt. Kailas is now considered the most important headstream of the Brahmaputra River. This region, one of the most remote and inaccessible in Tibet, was explored by the Swede Sven Hedin in 1907.*

150-151 *The Brahmaputra's valley, which runs through Tibet like a huge scar for over 745 miles (1200 km), is surrounded by a high-altitude desert. The formation of the Himalayas changed the river's course; it once flowed westward.*

151 bottom This Tibetan woman is drawing water from a pool at the headwaters of the Brahmaputra. After the Chinese invasion, which imposed social modes quite alien to the traditional local culture, many Tibetans sought refuge in neighboring countries.

THE BRAHMAPUTRA

quantity of silt that has been estimated at about 600 million tons per year. In its course, which is not attenuated by bends or meanders, the Tsang-po is always at an altitude of around 13,200 ft (4000 m), which makes it the highest river in the world. As is only fit for the young son of a god, this river is unpredictable and capricious: its course is unstable, its dimensions change suddenly, with incredible speed, jeopardizing the property and very life of the people who live along its shores. The erosive action of the river is violent and relentless, and is augmented by the frequent earthquakes that strike this region; the risk of uncontrollable floods is constant and serious. Like a huge, frothy braid, the bed of the Brahmaputra shifts and widens continuously, ruining cultivated fields and villages alike. The floods often occur suddenly and unexpectedly, caused by glacier tributaries and above all by the monsoon rains that fall abundantly in the eastern regions of India from June to September: in the years when rainfall is particularly persistent and heavy, almost one-third of Bangladesh is flooded. During the catastrophic flood of 1988 the high water receded only 24 days later, killing hundreds of people and undermining the already fragile local economy.

After passing through the city of Xiqaze and near the Tashilumpo monastery, the traditional residence of the Panchen Lama, the Tsang-po proceeds without incidents up to the village of Gyala. Here to block its passage toward the ocean are the last colossal mountains of the Himalaya range, the Namcha Barwa and Gyala Pera, which are well over 23,000

152 top This view of the valley of the Brahmaputra, which in Tibet is called the Tsang-po, highlights the configuration of a terrain that has changed due to the tectonic movements so common in this region.

152 center and bottom Wedged between the Himalayan range and the southern edge of the Tibet plateau, the Brahmaputra flows swiftly in a broad, very straight valley.

153 bottom right Flowing in a bed with indefinite margins, the Brahmaputra appears to be placid, as shown here. But in reality the river is notorious for sudden and violent floods that can change its configuration with lightning speed.

152-153 Fields and hills border this section of the Brahmaputra, which is swollen because of the spring thaw. From Tibet to the plains of Bangladesh, there is an incredible variety in the scenery by the river.

153 bottom left In the most remote regions of Tibet, people travel on the Brahmaputra with boats consisting of a wooden framework covered with yak hides.

160 top The pyramid of Mt. Shivling towers over the glaciers that are the headstreams of the Ganges River in the Indian state of Uttar Pradesh. Mt. Shivling, like Nanda Devi and the other peaks in the vicinity, is considered a sacred mountain.

160 bottom Indifferent to the cold, a pilgrim contemplates the Ganges, which makes its way through the ice that covers the slopes of the western Himalayas. The river's main sources are at an altitude of almost 16,400 ft (5000 m).

160-161 A fissure in the Gangotri glacier, known as the 'Cow's Mouth,' is the headstream of the sacred Ganges, which a short distance farther on flows into a narrow, snow-covered valley. The tall Bhagirathi Peaks can be seen clearly in the background.

Deccan mountains: the immense, flooded basin gradually filled with river silt, thus forming the present-day Ganges plain.

Indian mythology suggests a theory that is equally satisfying, at least from a spiritual standpoint. According to the sacred Hindu texts, the divine Ganga, invoked by the old ascetic Bhagirathi, descended from the heavens to resuscitate with her waters the 60,000 sons of a king who had been reduced to ashes because of an evil spell. However, during her torrential descent Ganga overran the Earth itself and destroyed all humankind. Only Shiva could stem the overwhelming power of the current. Moved by the interminable prayers of Bhagirathi, who for 1000 years called upon him with a superhuman vow of asceticism, Shiva agreed to entrap Ganga in the maze of his braided hair. Another supplication on the part of the pious

Bhagirathi persuaded the god to free Ganga, who was now under control, so that she finally flow on the Earth and fulfill her mission of purification. For millions of Indians, physical contact with the Ganges brings about total regeneration; it means purifying oneself from sin and taking a few steps closer to the infinite. In the many images of Ganga, the goddess is sometimes portrayed in the guise of an adolescent and at other times as a mature and shapely woman who is often riding a mythical animal with a fish's tail and the head of an elephant. Her gaze and features always express peace and wisdom. An extensive series of holy places accompanies the long journey of the Ganges from its source to the outlet in the Bay of Bengal. The goddess Ganga is revered throughout India, as can be seen by the numerous temples and shrines dedicated to her.

THE GANGES

The river leaves the mountains for good at Hardwar, about 434 miles (700 km) below Gangotri, and enters the great plain, which it will cross for the following 1240 miles (2000 km) of its course. The Ganges then makes a broad bend toward the south and reaches Allahabad, where it merges with the Jumna River, its twin. The interfluvial land (known as doab) between the almost parallel Ganges and Jumna is extremely fertile. Since the beginning of human history the rich and productive Ganges plain has been the key factor in the economic and political control of the subcontintent. The Indo-Aryans, Hindus, Muslims and European colonizers established and consolidated their fortune on the banks of the river, leaving impressive testimony of their power. Allahabad is not only the site where the Ganges and Jumna merge; there is also a third flux, this time spiritual and invisible, that adds its energy to the sacred Ganges: this subterranean current, which the Indians call Sarasvati, is an indispensable element of the divine trinity. Every twelve years, on occasion of the Kumbh Mela feast, Allahabad is invaded by immense crowds of worshippers who fill every corner of the city, moving ceaselessly among the temples and shrines in search of hope of redemption. Each of these holy places has a particular symbolic meaning: all the many Indian gods have passed through Allahabad, leaving a sign of their presence. And all of them are venerated. Perhaps only Varanasi (Benares), in the Ganges plain, can vie with Allahabad as the site of such a profound mystical quest.

In the long section that crosses Uttar Pradesh, the river passes through important and densely populated towns, but

162 top A procession of worshippers of the goddess Ganga crosses one of the bridges over the Ganges at Allahabad, in the Uttar Pradesh region, on occasion of the Kumbh Mela, the most important Hindu religious feast in India.

162 center A series of pontoon bridges built expressly for the many pilgrims connects the two banks of the Ganges at Allahabad during the Kumbh Mela festivities. In 2001 about 30 million people gathered in the city.